Smoky Mountain Memories

Smoky Mountain
Memories

Stories from the Hearts of Dolly Parton's Family

Willadeene Parton

RUTLEDGE HILL PRESS
Nashville, Tennessee

Published in Nashville, Tennessee, by Rutledge Hill Press, 211 Seventh Avenue North, Nashville, Tennessee 37219. Distributed in Canada by H. B. Fenn & Company, Ltd., 1090 Lorimar Drive, Mississauga, Ontario L5S 1R7. Distributed in Australia by Millenium Books, 13/3 Maddox Street, Alexandria NSW 2015. Distributed in New Zealand by Tandem Press, 2 Rugby Road, Birkenhead, Auckland 10. Distributed in the United Kingdom by Verulam Publishing, Ltd., 152A Park Street Lane, Park Street, St. Albans, Hertfordshire AL2 2AU.

Typography by Harriette Bateman, Bateman Design, Nashville, Tennessee.

Photographs on pages xii, xvii, xviii, 51, and 176 by Geoffrey D. Stone. Photograph on page 157 by Harriette Bateman.

Lyrics on page 198 are from THAT WAS A RIVER, words and music by Rick Giles and Susan Longacre, © 1992 Great Cumberland Music, Diamond Struck Music, Patenrick Music, WB Music Corp., and Long Acre Music. All rights reserved. Used by permission. WARNER BROS. PUBLICATIONS U.S. INC., Miami, FL 33014.

ISBN 1-55853-404-0

In loving memory of
my late husband, Raymond.

Contents

Introduction

*I*f only my brothers and sisters and I had known that our oldest sister, Willadeene, would grow up to write a book about us, we might have been a little nicer to her when we were younger. She was always the quiet one who never told on us, no matter what, and now, too late, we know why! She was only saving up so she could tell the whole wide world!

Willadeene, though not much older than me, always seemed more like a mother to us than a sister. Since she was the first-born in our family of twelve she seemed, somehow, to feel totally responsible for the rest of us. She was always willing to help us, always ready to defend us, and always quick to encourage us. In fact, I just might very well owe my success in life to her. They say that when I was just a little baby, Mama put my crib in the yard and told Willadeene to watch me while Mama went about her washing. Willadeene, being the little mother, decided she would pick me up and toss me into the air like she had seen Daddy and Mama do. Well, since she was a little girl who only thought she was big, she dropped me on my head and let me roll down a steep hill, all the way to the wash house where Mama was working. They say I wasn't hurt, but I always tell Willadeene that she gave me a head start in life and that I've been on a roll ever since!

I am really proud of my family. I often say on stage, when I'm introducing a song, that I sing about the hard times. We had no money growing up, but we had all the things that money can't buy—the good stuff—like love, kindness, understanding, and enough faith to move the Smoky Mountains. It was our faith in God and our love for each other that pulled us through things you would think there was no getting out of. There was also our music, which, next to God and family, was the strongest force in our lives.

For years Willadeene has wanted to write a book about our family, believing that our people were worth writing about. So, one day, she finally picked up her pencil and paper and, with her mountain honesty, down-to-earth humor, country sweetness, and straightforward southern style, she decided to make you part of our family. In this book she shares with you our favorite family memories and Smoky Mountain tall tales, which lead me to stretch the truth even to this day. She also makes you part of our hopes and fears . . . our laughter and tears . . . the best and the worst . . . the even unheard of . . . the quite unbelievable . . . the almost unspeakable. Who does she think she is, telling secrets? Family secrets! She's dragged everybody into it—friends, enemies, neighbors, uncles, aunts, cousins, Mama and Daddy, grandparents, great-great-grandparents, and so on down the line. If only my brothers and sisters and I had known. I mean, just because she's beautiful, talented, and intelligent, with a charming personality, doesn't mean we're gonna let her get away with it! For now we'll just let her look good (at our expense) and hope she makes a million dollars (and splits it with us) but, more than anything else, all kidding aside, we hope she shows how very much we all love and appreciate her and how very proud we are of her and how very glad we are to walk with her in the shadow of a song.

—Dolly Parton

Editor's Introduction

$\mathcal{P}$igeon Forge is a bustling tourist town—full of malls and rides, motels and restaurants reflecting the glow of neon. I turned off the parkway onto Upper Middle Creek Road. Within a couple of minutes I was leaving behind the neon glow of the town. Soon the only lights I saw were in the windows of rural homes and those haloing an occasional small frame church.

I was headed deep into rural Sevier County on my way to Caton's Chapel, the home of Willadeene Parton and the center of the Parton family's world. I had come to work with Willadeene on this book, and it was my first trip to her home in East Tennessee. I didn't know what to expect, but I should have. It was all right there in the manuscript.

For many years I have admired Dolly Parton's musical gifts—especially her songwriting. Hers is a poetry of memory, rooted deep in the mountains and hill country of East Tennessee and springing from the sometimes fierce independence of southern mountain folk. But until I had the opportunity and privilege to work with Willadeene Parton on this book I did not know the extraordinary Parton *family*, whose lives embody and personify the struggles, pain, joy, and comfort of growing up in the mountains of the rural South during a time when America was different than it is now.

My literal passage—from the neon of Pigeon Forge to the home of the Parton family—is a metaphor for Willadeene's story and her message. In a very real sense what has changed about the world in which the Parton children grew up is not what is important about Willadeene's story. The *rhythm of memory*—what was, what is, what will be, what will not change—is the soul, the sustaining heart of Willadeene's story.

Willadeene, the eldest child of the Parton clan, is a warm and gracious woman. Her family is quite talented, but she has a very special gift—a unique

Statue of Dolly on the courthouse square in Sevierville.

literary voice. She can tell the story of her family in a way that communicates the specialness of that family and its experiences while at the same time she taps into our common experience of family and the *rhythm of memory*.

The Sevier County of Willadeene's childhood has in a sense disappeared: the poolroom on Bruce Street—a place of ominous mystery to the Parton girls—is long gone; the whittlers and knife traders who populated the courthouse square are no longer there. In fact, the courthouse square now features a statue of Dolly. The dusty road from Sevierville to Pigeon Forge has been replaced by a six-lane highway that is usually clogged with cars and campers and trucks.

Willadeene does not "sugarcoat." Times were hard. Mother Parton was often sick, and it fell to Willadeene to take care of her younger brothers and sisters. She lost part of her childhood—she gained much and gave much. And finally, that is the story. None of the Partons would be who or what they are without the whole, entire Parton *family*. The strength of that cohesive unit and loving circle allowed this family of extraordinarily talented individuals to move into a "modern" world without ever losing the love *of* their family or the love *for* their family. And it goes on. Thank God.

I am personally grateful that this book has given me an opportunity to come to know and love Willadeene. She is a wise and generous woman. "Deene" has become my friend and the big sister I've always wished for. I think that as you come to know her and her family through this book you will, as I have, become a little envious of a family that grew up rich in all the things that matter.

—Charla Honea, *March 1996*

Author sitting by a mountain stream.

Preface

To hold a piece of yesterday
Wrapped in wondrous glow
Is the greatest gift that I can give you
And the greatest joy I know.

I still live in Sevier County, Tennessee, the place where my family grew up. Sevier County itself is typical of the southern mountains, but the way its inhabitants live is different from most other parts of the country. Even in today's technological age we jealously guard our mountain heritage and work hard to maintain our old ways and culture. East Tennessee is a strange combination of computers and cornfields, atomic plants and outside toilets, tourism and tent revivals, breeder reactors and barnyards.

We know that necessary advancements of civilization are a part of our daily lives and we tolerate them, but deep within ourselves, we don't want to accept them. We live and work in a society that didn't come about gradually, but was thrust upon us so quickly that we can't adjust. So we hold onto the security of mountain ways, because the familiarity of what we know best and the pride derived from that knowledge have strengthened and sustained us in a seemingly cluttered, mad, racing world.

We cling to simple pleasures—crisp winter days, the beauty of the morning mist, the dew of dusk. We cling to the soft, pure mountain dialect of our people, even though the words and accent particular to this area are slowly dying out. We are learning "proper" English from television, teachers from other states, and the great influx of tourists who come to our area. Most important, we cling to and honor our childhoods and the days of doing nothing but growing up.

We grew up in a world where the only time we had to rush was to get the mown hay into the barn, to get the clothes off the line before it rained, to run the cattle out of the cornfield, to take someone to the doctor, or just to get home before dark.

Nature decided when things would be done. The seasons decreed the time to plant, the time to harvest. Our lives were governed by nature, and nature is never in a hurry. We worked hard, lived close to the land, and had great respect for the earth we loved.

The people of Sevier county have always been focused on their families and claim kin as far as we can trace them, even unto fifth and sixth cousins. It's not unusual to hear someone say, "Yeah, we're a'kinned. His great-grandmother's uncle on his father's side married my great-great-grandmother's sister." When family reunions are held, it's not just the immediate family that attend, but people so remotely related that it's hard to trace the relationship. There is a closeness, a family pride, and a warm security in knowing you're part of a clan of loving people, that you're a part of such a wide, caring circle.

Then there are those who are not related by blood but by a deep love for a family. Someone asked a man in his late sixties who attended a family reunion, "Now, how are you a'kinned?"

"Oh, we're not," he said. "But your granddaddy took my father in when his daddy died, cause his mama couldn't feed them all. So he went to stay with him and helped out on the farm for his keep. I'll never forget it. Your granddaddy just barely had enough to get by on, but he kept my father's mother and the little ones from starving. Every Saturday he made Dad go home and take a tow sack full of food to his family. It's something you don't forget."

So the love goes on and spills over into generation after generation, and the remembering by that man's family creates a bond that will last through the years and through his children's children and later generations.

Our family is very close, but we're also very different. We enjoy our unique differences and want to maintain the freedom and joy of being who and what we are. We like the way we live, and we love our special county and its people.

How many people have lived as people did a hundred years ago and also have been exposed to people and cultures from all over the world through travel in their work? When we were young, we didn't know about skyscrapers, but we knew where the May apples grew. We'd never seen a streetcar, but we knew how to make lye soap. We'd never heard an orchestra, but we'd watched

The beautiful Smoky Mountains.

An old covered bridge in Sevier County.

bobcat kittens play. We'd never seen an ostrich, but we had a pet crow that talked. We didn't have hothouse orchids, but we had mountain laurel and lady's slippers. We didn't wear fashionable clothes, but we knew the taste of mountain teaberries.

Many years have passed since our childhood days, but the mountains are the same. Deep within their hollows lies the land that contains the graves of our ancestors and kin. Their only markings are gray slate rocks for headstones. The name, date of birth, and date of death are sometimes scratched on the rock, sometimes not.

I have spent days tracing my ancestors and walking among the ruins of farms and empty fields that once belonged to kin I've never known. Scattered through the trees and close to the rotting logs and tumbled-down chimneys are old lichen-covered peach and plum trees still blooming and bearing their fruit year after year. Here the white-tailed deer feed undisturbed on still, autumn days, and yellow jackets and hornets lazily hollow out the insides of rotting fruit on the ground.

How fortunate we are to be able to retrace our roots and walk in the footprints left empty years ago. Recently I went back to one of the places where we lived when we were growing up. Not much was left, except a sagging plank house and a rusty tin roof with the corners turned up so that they flapped when the wind stirred. I walked up the rotting steps and saw, after all these years, on what was left of the screen door, a spool that Mother had nailed there for a handle.

It was then that memories of the bad times, the good times, the laughter, and the tears engulfed me. It was as if time reversed itself and came around the mountain, bringing my childhood to blindside me. It was then and there that I decided to write this book to record the memories before they were lost.

I have good memories and sad ones. I find now that as I move through the seasons of the years, these memories and stories become especially vibrant and poignant. It may be the hammering of a woodpecker, the crackle of winter ice, or the dusty heat of a summer day, but I find myself stringing these memories on a golden chain in my heart. I have written them down so you can join us in our ups and downs, our happiness and woe.

Welcome to my family!

—Willadeene Parton, *January 1996*

In the Shadow of a Song

Words and Music by
WILLADEENE PARTON

In the shad - ow of a song, Life was hard,

love was strong. Hand in hand we walked a - long so proud to -

geth - er _____ In the shad-ow of a song. _____

Smok - y Moun - tain mem - o - ries in my dreams I can see

A cab - in in the hills where we played and Ma - ma told us sto - ries

In the shad - ow of a song. _____ We walk to -

geth - er in the shad - ow of a song. _____ Love will live for -

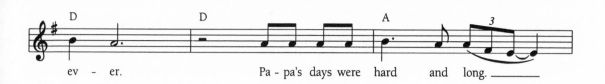

ev - er. Pa - pa's days were hard and long. _____

He had to work from dawn till dusk. _____

In the shad - ow of a song, in these hills where we were born.

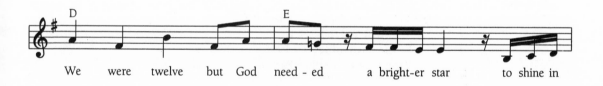

We were twelve but God need - ed a bright-er star to shine in

heav - en. _____ Now there's e - lev - en. _____

CODA

In the shad-ow of a song _____ we walk to - geth - er,

In the shad-ow of a song _____ love will live for - ev - er.

Genealogy

George Washington Rayfield
(1854–1935), son of Charles Rayfield
and Elizabeth Bohannon;
married in 1875 to
Cassie Ann Moore (1860–1934),
daughter of Andy Moore and
Rachel Metcalf.
Daughter Bessie Elizabeth.

Albert Huston Parton
(1865–1930), son of
Benjamin Christopher Parton and
Margaret Evans; married in 1888 to
Tennessee "Tenny" S. Russell
(1872–1954), daughter of Larendan D.
Russell and Hannah Downs.
Parents of William Walter Parton.

William Walter Parton (1888–1982);
married in 1912 to
Bessie Rayfield (1898–1975).
Parents of Robert Lee Parton.

Lloyd Henry Valentine
(1874–1947); married in 1898 to
Louisa Margaret Whitted (1880–1960).
Parents of Rena Kansas.

James Robert Owens
(1877–1940), son of
Samuel Paxton Owens and Annie Sutton;
married in 1889 to
Mary Melinda Messer (1880–1959),
daughter of Isaac A. Messer and
Nancy Conard.
Parents of Jacob Robert
(Reverend Jake) Owens.

Reverend Jacob Robert Owens
(1899–1992); married in 1919 to
Rena Kansas Valentine (1902–1968).
Parents of Avie Lee Owens Parton

Robert Lee Parton married Avie Lee Caroline Owens in 1939.

Their children and spouses:

Willadeene: first marriage to Arthur Blalock, Jr. (divorced)
child: Mitchell Blaine
second marriage to Raymond Joseph Buzzeo, Jr. (deceased)

David Wilburn: first marriage to Maggie Ann (Pat) Maples (divorced)
children: Donna Lee, Donnie David (deceased), and Cassie Dena
second marriage to Kaye McCoig

Coy Denver: married to Carolyn Parton (not related)
children: Dolly Christina and Jennifer Lynn

Dolly Rebecca: married to Carl Dean

Bobby Lee: first marriage to Doris Noland (divorced)
children: Clint Warren and Danielle Cleon
second marriage to Angie McGaha

Stella Mae: married to Carroll Rauhuff (divorced)
child: Timothy Carroll

Cassie Nan: married to Larry Seaver
children: Bryan Melvin and Rebecca Ann Keikilani

Randy Huston: married to Debra (Deb) Humphrey
children: Tever Louise and Heidi Lou

Larry Garrold (died at birth)

Freida Estelle: married to Mark Andersen (divorced)
child: Jada Star

Floyd Estel

Rachel Ann: married to Richard Dennison
child: Hannah Raquelle

Acknowledgments

I want to acknowledge my son, Mitchell Blalock, my parents, and my brothers and sisters—David, Denver, Dolly, Bobby, Stella, Cassie, Randy, Freida, Floyd, and Rachel. Then there's Joan McCullah. The help, faith, and encouragement of these people gave me the courage to begin again, to write and to publish. They have all participated by remembering new and old stories they thought should be told. They have corrected, scolded, laughed at, cried about, and acted out many of these memories. Without their intrusion there would be no book. They have always allowed me to spend many hours at my work, because they consider my writing a special gift. This book is also in loving memory of my brother Larry.

Thanks to Wayne Ball, who has been considered a best friend to most of the family for more than forty years. Several of the girls have had crushes on him at one time or another. He says I'm the one he always wanted—yeah, right. To Barb, who has done so much for so many, thank you. Your day will come.

Other Acknowledgments

Special thanks go to all the people who gave me stories, helped me with birth, wedding, and death dates and photographs: the staff of Dollywood, Dennis Carney, Darrell Bradley, Shirley Flynn, Joan Shortt, Juli Dorland, Larry Miller, Ruth Whitted, Lisa Dowling, Hope Powell, Roger Harron, Olan Mills, Glamour Shots, Cathy Parton, Doris Parton, Doris N. Parton (genealogy and mountain verse), Linda and Karl Lewanski (*The Star Journal*), Lillie O. Huskey, Neva, Vita Wilson King (Mountain Press), Bob Childress (Mountain Press), Terry Morrow (Mountain Press), Nancy Clabo, Cheryl Carpenter, Brenda Madden, George Kuffrey, Ricke Hester, and Jacque King.

Other special people I want to acknowledge are David Taylor, Shelby Lester, Heeya So, Billy, Sabin, and Rena Conley.

In my special memories are Regina "Maw" Taylor, Marion Clark, Edward Nave, and Dora Valentine.

Autumn

Autumn!
Quickly, catch the magic!
Hold it tight!
It's getting away!
Don't you hear Jack Frost tiptoeing
across the lovely meadow,
pointing his icy fingers at the
already bowing, faded gray heads
of the thistle and meadowlace?
The goldenrod and the asters,
the purple ironweed,
the blue and white frost flowers
are all waiting to be taken
by the cold, along with the soft blue chickweed that covers
the soon-to-be-bare fields.
Roadside signs with vines covering them
will soon be bare, so we can see
what they say again.
The old barn, leaning almost into the road,
is covered with honeysuckle.
A few blossoms remain in tiny bunches
with the leaves underneath them
like soft beds to rest upon.
The Lombardy poplar, with its young
sprouts all around,
looks like a father with many children,
who just realized he had so many.
You did real well, Autumn.
You held on such a long time,
but last night you let go.
I guess you grew tired
and went to sleep for a moment,
and the frost blew its icy breath,
cold and fresh, on my world.
He drew marvelous pictures
on all the windows, even the
stained-glass ones in the church,
and I saw the gravestone with
crystal-covered ivy vines
in the graveyard.

God and church were as much a part of our daily lives as breathing. It wasn't "religion" to be practiced at church, but a natural faith that was and is part of our everyday living and thinking. Although we were isolated more than families are today, Mother saw to it that we knew who God is and what He can do. She believed it was her duty to teach us and she did her duty, not only for her children but for her grandchildren as well.

She lived her beliefs daily, so we grew up never separating God from any other aspects of our lives. We were taught what evil and sin were, and not doing something to help someone who needed it was a sin.

Mother stressed that before we did anything, we'd better stop and think if we wanted to answer for it; because everything we did was written down in Heaven, and on Judgment Day, when our names were called, we'd have to account for all of it. We weren't taught religion, we were taught faith and the Ten Commandments and how to live the way God requires us to.

The little church Grandpa Jake started. Papa and some of his brothers helped build it. We went to church there while we were growing up.

Front row (left to right): Stella, Mother, Rachel, Papa, and Cassie. *Back row (left to right):* Randy, Dolly, me, Denver, Floyd, Bobby, Freida, and David.

Mother's faith is so pure and childlike that I think if God didn't answer one of her prayers she'd be totally shocked. She holds to the promises made in the Bible: "Ask, and it shall be given you" (Matthew 7:7). "And all things, whatsoever ye shall ask in prayer, believing, ye shall receive" (Matthew 21:22). "Therefore I say unto you, what things soever ye desire, when ye pray, believe that ye receive them, and ye shall have them" (Mark 11:24). We were taught there is nothing God can't do. If God can create us, He certainly can heal us.

Randy was born with an open valve in his heart. For years Mother took him to a heart specialist who told her Randy wouldn't live beyond his teens. But Mother refused to accept that and nine-year-old Randy believed what Mother

Papa with all his favorite girls except Dolly.

taught: "When ye pray, believe, . . . and ye shall have them." Randy would go to church and when it was almost time to close the worship service with singing or at the altar call, he would whisper to Grandpa Jake or Aunt Dorothy Jo, "Don't forget the healing services."

Randy was healed at church. Mother wasn't there that night; he came running in the house and cried, "Mama, I got healed!" She asked, "How do you know, Randy?" He said, "It felt like fire going through my chest when they prayed for me." "What kind of fire?" Randy answered, "A warm fire, Mama." Later when the doctor examined Randy, he confirmed that the valve was repaired, just like he'd had open-heart surgery. Yes, we believe. . . .

Mother has almost died twice, once from spinal meningitis and the other time from a miscarriage. We were at school the day Mother miscarried. Bobby and Stella weren't old enough to go to school. Mother sent five-year-old Bobby to the school to bring us home. It must have been a long, long walk for such a little boy. He walked through a field of cattle that even the older kids were afraid of, and he carried a stick for protection. When he got to the schoolhouse, he just stood in the door, tired and scared and trying not to cry.

When I saw him, I knew something was very wrong. I ran to him and knelt down and put my arms around him. He tried to be strong. "Willadeene, come home. Mama's sick." Then he cried, "Oh, Willadeene, she's so sick and there's blood. . . ."

We gathered David, Denver, and Dolly and ran home. Mother was lying in a blood-soaked bed. She was hemorrhaging so badly that the blood had soaked through the thin mattress and was dripping on the floor. Stella was on the bed with Mother, crying because she was so afraid.

Mother lay still, holding her Bible close to her chest. Stella remembers Mother praying until she was too weak to speak aloud. She told Stella to get her Bible. Three-year-old Stella climbed up on a straight-backed, twine-bottomed chair. She got the Bible from the mantel over the fireplace and then climbed back into the bed beside Mother.

David and Denver rode our horse to Grandma Rena's for help and then to get Papa. It seemed like a long time before we saw Grandma Rena and Aunt Ora (Grandma Rena's sister) running toward the house. Finally the ambulance from Atchley's Funeral Home arrived at the schoolhouse, which was as close as a car could get to our house. They put Mother on the stretcher, and Papa helped carry her to the ambulance. We stood on the porch and watched as they carried our mother the half-mile through the sedge field to the school-house. Mother was in the hospital a long time, and we were ecstatic when she came home, even though she was still bent over and very frail.

I was eleven years old, and I will never forget the overwhelming fear of realizing Mother might die. This experience deepened my appreciation for every member of my family.

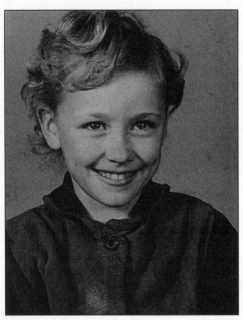

Dolly in her coat of many colors.

This past fall a sudden cascade of leaves reminded me of one sunny October afternoon long ago when I was five years old, and multicolored leaves covered the ground. Squirrels hurried about gathering the last of summer's fruit and nuts, and our black-and-white shepherd dog, Frisky, lay near the door of our log cabin.

My mother and her mother, Grandma Rena, and three neighbor ladies were sitting on our front porch talking. Mother and Grandma sat in the swing, which Mother pushed with her foot from time to time.

My brothers David and Denver and our uncle, Alden Owens, a couple of years older than us, and myself were in the yard building mounds of leaves, then jumping into them, laughing as they flew over the yard once again. After a while we got bored, as usual.

Alden and David wondered about one of the neighbor lady's ears being so big. Alden knew better than to ask. I was more concerned about why Mother's tummy was so fat. David and I walked up the steps to the porch, and after a lot of encouragement from Alden, we finally asked our questions.

For my effort I got scolded by everyone on the porch. But David wasn't so

Left to right: Randy, Dolly, Stella, Denver, Cassie, David, Rachel, and Floyd. They must have saved the space for Freida.

lucky—or so tactful. He was standing close to Grandma and looking up at the lady. He asked her why she had ears like a donkey. David, Alden, and I still laugh at how that bunch of women carried on even after Grandma had spanked him.

Mother got up from the swing and walked into the house. I saw a smile on her face as she passed me. She was only twenty-one, already had three children, and was expecting another one soon— Dolly Rebecca.

My infant son, Mitchell, and me in 1962.

*D*uring the years when we were little, school started in the fall about the time persimmons, honey locusts, and Winter John apples were getting ripe. We ate them when they were ripe enough, but all the children at school fought and hit each other with the green persimmons as soon as school started.

Freida was always Rachel's ally and self-appointed protector. Rachel was quiet and didn't like trouble of any kind, but Freida wasn't quiet and she loved a good argument. When Rachel first started school, if anyone picked a fight with her, she'd tell them, "Oh, Freida doesn't let me fight, she fights for me!"

We usually had a few choice fighting buddies, whom we could always depend on for a good fight. One evening we were coming home from school and our enemies were spoiling for a fight. It was awful! We were outnumbered and, of course, we got whipped. Dolly and Denver had seen the fight coming and ran all the way home, leaving David and me to fight it out.

When we got home and told Mother what happened, she shook Dolly and

Barefoot school days. *Front row (right to left):* second child Bobby. *Second row (right to left):* first child Dolly. Most children went barefoot because it felt good, but some did because they had no shoes.

Willadeene

David

Bobby

Dolly

Stella

Twins, Floyd and Freida

Denver

Randy

Rachel

Cassie

Denver and said, "Why did you run off from David and Willadeene?" They said, "But, Mama, we didn't, we were coming home anyway!"

Some days we and our fighting buddies would stop on our way home from school and sit under the catalpa tree in their backyard and smoke the "Indian cigars" from the tree. We often copied Mother and Papa in their tobacco habits. We would smoke "rabbit tobacco" (a wild herb) because we'd learned that the real tobacco made us deathly sick (and still does, most of us). We loved chocolate, so we'd mix powdered Hershey's cocoa with sugar and play like it was snuff. Real snuff is powdered tobacco that is placed between the lower lip and gum. It gives the same effect as chewing tobacco, but you don't have to chew. A dip of snuff is the amount you can hold comfortably in your lip. We'd fill up Mother's empty Levi Garrett snuff cans with our chocolate snuff and pretend to be real tough. We never spit because we liked our "snuff" too much to waste it. Sometimes, we'd just use the plain cocoa without sugar. This didn't happen often, only when we felt real mean and tough. You had to be tough if you dipped cocoa straight because it was very bitter.

Papa, Freida, and Randy at a recent Apple Festival in Sevierville.

For years in the fall we girls would go "hunting" with the boys, and our dog Brownie always went along to flush the rabbits and birds out of their hiding places. The boys really didn't like for us to go with them, but we loved to tag along, just to aggravate them.

Many days we hunted pine knots to start fires back at home in the fireplace and the wood stove. These knots were so rich with resin that a fire could be started by lighting a few shavings off them, and we wouldn't even have to use coal oil.

We also would cut resin from the pine trees to make chewing gum, but first it had to be melted before we could chew it. We would take the lid off a Bob White syrup jar and put the resin in the lid and set it on the back of the old wood cookstove to melt. It was especially good if you mixed real chewing gum with it.

While we were out in the woods, we girls would gather holly branches, because they were so pretty, and pine boughs, because they smelled good. We always enjoyed having natural beauty from the woods to brighten up the house.

Sometimes at night the boys and Papa would go possum hunting. They would reluctantly let us girls go with them because they needed someone to carry the coffee and biscuits filled with peppered, fried potatoes, home-cured bacon, or ham. We hated to have to carry everything, but we loved to go hunting in the dark. Not too far into the hunting trip, we would stop and eat our picnic in the moonlight. Then we girls would gladly return to warmth of the house while Papa and the boys continued their nocturnal adventures.

~

After school started and the crops were "laid-by" (the time between hoeing the ground for the last time and the harvest), our local church would hold a revival. School would let out about nine-thirty and the teachers would line us up. We all would march to the church house for the ten o'clock services. As we walked to church, we would sing "Walking in the Light" and "I

Cassie and me with a trophy at Fan Fair.

Shall Not Be Moved." After sitting through two hours of revival services we would then march back to school for a long recess and have classes the rest of the day.

Our first audiences for our family's music and singing were church congregations. We were very young, and our voices had not developed yet.

I remember when Freida and Floyd were six years old and Rachel was four. They were caught up in Beatlemania. Now all the children who wanted to were allowed (even encouraged) to sing for the congregation, and most of them did. Freida, Floyd, and Rachel wanted to surprise everyone with a new

Beautiful sister Cassie at Dolly's booth at Fan Fair. Cassie has worked for Dolly all her adult life.

version of "Jesus Loves Me." When it came their turn to sing, the small trio marched up to the front of the church. Their young voices rang out in perfect harmony, "Jesus loves me, this I know, yeah, yeah, yeah."

Cassie loved church. She was always quiet and helpful. She loved sweeping up and carrying chunks of coal for the stove. And she loved singing. One of Cassie's favorite songs was "Don't Doubt Me, Thomas, I Am the Man." One Sunday night, Stella and Cassie were singing the song. When they came to the line, "Look at my hands, Thomas, I am the man," they both held up their open hands to the audience. One pair of hands was clean—the other dirty. All the brothers and other sisters laughed, and Stella made Cassie hide her hands. Poor Cassie, disgraced at such a young age just because she had helped build the fire and forgot to wash her hands!

*W*hile he was in his mid teens, Randy went to work for Blalock Brothers Construction Company with his experienced brothers and Papa. After helping build a bridge and miles of highway, Randy suddenly decided to pursue a musical career. He had never played an instrument, but he told Dolly he really needed a bass guitar. When Randy would come home from work he'd rush to his room to practice the bass. Uncle Bill Owens helped him by writing out the music. Randy said the bass fit his hands a lot better than the pick and shovel ever did.

Randy's first show was in September 1974 at the Duck Inn in Maryville, Tennessee. Uncle Henry and Gene Shahan, who were playing there, got him the job. It was a honky-tonk. Uncle Henry told

Randy on the job at Dollywood. That mike fits his hand pretty well, too.

Left to right: Mother, Randy, Dolly, Floyd, and Freida. Part of the traveling family band.

Randy to play the songs in the key of E, but Randy was so nervous that he played every song in the key of A. He wasn't really ready to play professionally, but he was determined and persevered.

Randy began playing at a lot of truck stops after that. At one of the rougher ones a middle-aged lady, several pounds over-weight, wearing a blonde wig and black-rimmed glasses with one of the earpieces missing, told the band she wanted to sing. She wore a jersey, leopard-skin jumpsuit, and she looked like a king-sized pillow. There were two men with her. One had tattoos, and the other wore a hat with lots of feathers. He had a pack of cigarettes rolled up in the sleeve of his black shirt.

She sang Loretta Lynn's "You Ain't Woman Enough to Take My Man" while Randy and the band played for her. She said to Randy, "You know where I learned to sing?" Randy said, "No." "In the shower. It's the only place I've ever sung before tonight." She decided she and Randy should do a duet, but when she would suggest a song, he would say he did not know the words. Finally she said, "Damn it, you know 'On Top of Old Smoky,' don't you?" He finally gave in, and sang every word with her.

Back in the 1970s Dolly was playing an Elks lodge in Texas near the Mexican border. The first set went well. Randy was the front man, the emcee who opens the show and introduces the star. The band hadn't eaten yet, but when the audience started buying them tequila, they drank it. When the second show started, Randy said, "Welcome back to the Moose Club." The Elks got highly offended. Finally, he said, "Oh, hell, what's the big fuss? They both have horns, don't they?" Dolly thought about firing him the next day, but instead she gave him a firm talking to, as only Dolly can do.

In 1975, Randy started with RCA with a song called "Tennessee Born." He used to play anywhere he could get work. He and Floyd lived in an old farmhouse outside Nashville for two or three years, and they depended on Stella for good home-cooked meals. Randy would go to Stella's house to eat as soon as he got back in town. If she was on the road working, Darlene Williams (Stella's son Tim's babysitter) would fix Randy macaroni and cheese or some other country food he liked.

RANDY PARTON
Exclusively on RCA

RC/I Records and Tapes

A young Randy, when he was with RCA.

This October I was making a batch of corn bread for dinner, and I started thinking about how sometimes people go to great lengths to meet us Partons, to see how we live, what we wear, what kind of cars we drive, even what kinds of foods we like. The food question is the easiest one to answer. We like all kinds, especially the kinds our mother fixed for us while we were growing up. Potato cakes, so quick and simple: just mashed potatoes, salt, and pepper whipped with enough flour to form into patties and fry in hot grease. I put a finely cut onion in mine, so when any of the family drops by at mealtime, the aroma hits them in the yard and they are ready to eat. Fried green tomatoes: just slice, roll in flour, salt, and pepper, and cook the same as potato cakes. Cinnamon or chocolate rolls: biscuit or pie dough rolled thin like a pie crust, cut in wide strips, spread with butter, sugar, and cinnamon or cocoa; roll, slice, and bake; then drizzle with powdered sugar frosting or just powdered sugar.

Left to right: Mother, Uncle Lester, and Aunt Estelle in olden times.

Our favorite corn bread is nothing more than a cup of cornmeal mix (or self-rising meal and a spoonful of self-rising flour), a spoonful of oil or bacon grease, and enough milk to make a stiff batter. Put this into a small greased pan and bake until brown, about thirty minutes.

Everyone knows what stone soup is (the stone is optional). It's all the leftovers you have on hand: potatoes, onions, carrots, peppers, or whatever. Add salt and pepper and butter and enough water to make the soup liquid. Use your imagination.

As you can see, our mother didn't have a lot of time or a lot of money to put into our meals, but those foods remain some of our favorites even today.

If you prepare some of these foods, you'll have a tasty country meal ready in a hurry.

Many times people can't help but show their disappointment when they see our homes and the cars we drive. They would be even more surprised to learn that quite a few of us don't even have savings accounts or health insurance or retirement plans. It's certainly not because Dolly doesn't help her family (and we have more than a hundred "close" relatives). We work hard, but Dolly works the

Mother and Papa out on the town.

hardest of us all. And she has earned every penny she has. Dolly is truly the busiest and most generous person I know.

In our books, Dolly and I have told you all we wanted you to know about us over the years. We each remember things our own way. Now if you want a story without it being dressed up, ask Denver—one thing he won't do is lie. He won't even tell a fish tale or fib about his hunting dogs.

Such honesty goes way back with him. Dolly tells this story in her book, *My Life and Other Unfinished Business*. On one particular morning the teacher asked each child to stand and tell what he or she had eaten for breakfast. Dolly recalls:

As I sat waiting for my turn, I became more and more embarrassed about the fact that all we ever had for breakfast was biscuits and gravy. Other kids were having really glorious breakfasts, orange juice, bacon, waffles, corn flakes, and all kinds of things that seemed wonderful and luxurious. I hated my biscuits and gravy as well as our poverty. I was not above a creative stretching of the truth to get me out of an uncomfortable situation.

When it came my turn, I made up a list from what other kids had named off, all the things that sounded the most appealing. Oh, I had eggs, waffles, orange juice, sausage, and corn flakes—I went on even as I made up my own dream breakfast. I could feel Denver's eyes burning a hole in my back. I had forgotten he would be next in line! I knew he wouldn't lie, especially not to save me.

What is he going to do? I worried, even as I wrapped up my imaginary menu. I finished detailing a breakfast good enough for three rich kids, then sat down to await my fate at the hands of mean, hateful, honest Denver. I was going to be shown up as a liar—worse yet, a poor, gravy-and-biscuit-eating liar. "And what did you have, Denver?" asked the teacher. I cringed. He stood up quickly and said simply, "I had what she had." This, of course, was the truth. He had in fact had the same pitiful biscuits and gravy I had. For a few moments I allowed myself to think that my brother had actually come to my rescue in a tight spot. But his fist pushed into my back and a hissed whisper of "liar" reminded me I was living in one of my dream worlds.

Front row (left to right): Bobby, Stella, and Cassie; center, Dolly. *Back row:* me, David, Denver, and Randy.

Above: Owens-Parton family gathering. *Front row (left to right):* Cassie, Uncle Lester, Cousin Donna Faye. *Second row (left to right):* Stella, Cousin Dale Denver, Bobby and Dolly *(standing in front of Mother). Third row (left to right):* Grandma Rena, Grandpa Jake, Aunt Estelle, David, me, Aunt Dorothy Jo, and Mother.

Left: This picture of Dolly looks very much like our mother—the dimples, the smile, the eyes.

$\mathcal{M}$y sisters and I have fond memories of the harvest festivals of our youth. Harvest festivals and pie suppers were held in the fall to raise money for school projects such as class trips, basketball team uniforms, or special equipment for science projects. All the women and girls of the community made the best pies and cakes they could. As the women brought in the pies, each pie was numbered so only the one who numbered the pies and its baker knew who the pie belonged to. Then it was put on the table with the rest of the numbered pies. Some women made the pies just to help the school and to show off their baking. Almost always these women would give their pie to a girl whose family couldn't afford the extra expense of the ingredients.

The single girls and women hoped their boyfriends or some boy they were secretly in love with would buy their pie, because whoever bought the pie had to eat it with the person who had baked it.

The cakes were judged, and first-, second-, and third-place ribbons were awarded for the prettiest cakes. These cakes were used as prizes in the cakewalk and other contests. The pie auction was the last event of the evening.

After the cakewalk we had "prettiest girl" and "ugliest man" contests. The girls were nominated by someone paying a fee and then giving the name of the girl he thought was prettiest. The names were written on the blackboard, with the amount of money donated written next to them. The "ugliest man" contest worked the same way, except the nominees had to stand up in front of the room to be teased. They didn't have to be ugly, of course. Often it was just someone the neighbors liked to pick on. Nor did the girl have to actually *be* pretty. She could be a girl everyone liked, or whose parents had a lot of money, or who her husband or boyfriend *thought* was the prettiest. It was all in fun and people had a good time teasing their neighbors.

Mother has told us of the pie suppers when she was young, and how the young man who bought the pie got to walk the girl home—if he was lucky. Mother remembers walking home with Papa on a path through the woods where there were a lot of fallen rotting trees. She remembers the soft glow of foxfire and the big orange October moon and Papa's strong arm around her waist.

The prettiest girl for sure.

Oh, our aching backs. We were just about done with summer work at this time of year. The tobacco crops were sold in December. Then we bought shoes for winter and paid for the groceries we had bought on credit.

The cutting of the tobacco usually marked the beginning of harvest for our family. The tobacco crop seemed like a job that lasted all year; it almost does, for the tobacco bed is sown in February, and it is December before the tobacco is finally taken to the warehouse and sold. We gathered the harvest until we were bone weary. We worked, we fought, and we played.

We would pick buckets full of the beautiful wine-colored muscadines that grew on huge vines along the river. And we'd find the dark purple wild grapes and sit and eat them in the warm, lazy days of Indian summer.

The cane stripping and molasses making came next. Then we took up the potatoes, peanuts, and onions. We gathered the last of the crowder peas and beans, and then the popcorn and Indian corn. We gathered the field corn last, usually after a few big frosts. The horse would be hitched to a sled, and he would pull the corn back to the corn crib. We kids worked hard, and I know we helped quite a bit, but Papa did most of the work.

When we weren't working close to Papa, the boys would start teasing us girls, telling us we looked like speckled hounds because we had freckles. Or they'd call us palomino ponies, because we had square, straight teeth. They told us we were skinny or fat or whatever. Finally Papa would take pity on us and tell them, "Leave your sisters alone and get back to work!"

I guess we did look a sight in our old drab work clothes. Now that we are older, we do wear better "work clothes" (well, some of us do). We'd tell the guys that they looked like girls. They would say, "Too bad you'uns don't!" Of course, some of us girls had developed more than others at that point.

The boys were handsome but they didn't seem to know it or care. We girls have complexes to this day over the way our brothers treated us then, and we are still convinced that our brothers are better looking than any of us.

Our cow, Pet.

The other day, Mother reminded me of one of the most hated times of our younger days. When the Watkins or Raleigh men came by in the fall, she would buy all kinds of things, like red liniment, carbolic salve, and even some good things like lemon and butterscotch pie filling and vanilla flavoring.

In winter, the salesmen did not come, and Mother would send Papa to town to get Vicks salve, camphorated oil, nose drops, and sweet oil (for earaches). When Papa was going out the door to catch a ride with one of the neighbors, we would sit quiet and still, hoping with all our hearts (and some of us saying a silent prayer) that Mother wouldn't remember a certain something. But she always did.

She would throw panic into our hearts when she said, "Oh, and Lee, don't forget, you might as well get some spring tonic and castor oil in case you don't get back into town before spring."

About the only thing we dreaded about winter was Mother's doctoring. According to Mother, after a bout with the flu, we had to get rid of any germs

An old picture of the Watkins man.

that might still lurk in our bodies. Believe me, we didn't harbor flu germs or anything else after her dose of castor oil. Our tired little bodies were weak, but purified.

We didn't know what was in it, but once a year we got a dose of spring tonic, along with a dose of castor oil. Mother would line us up, and no matter how much we begged and cried and swore we didn't need it, she would make us take the tonic immediately followed by the castor oil.

Papa would be standing by to make sure that we swallowed. Then he would give each of us a drink of grapefruit juice and a piece of teaberry gum to cut the taste. Dolly and Denver tried to fool Mother and Papa, but they never succeeded.

Then we would all sit around wide-eyed and still, waiting for what we knew was sure to come, and we knew we had to be ready to run at the first twinge. Sometimes we'd fight over the one seat in the outhouse, and the loser had the choice of seeking refuge in the woodshed or behind the smokehouse.

Here are a few other home remedies we used growing up:

FRECKLES RIDDANCE

Papa used to tell us to wash our faces in the morning dew, to get rid of our freckles. Every spring and summer, for a couple of weeks, my sisters and I would faithfully wash our faces in the morning dew at dawn. I don't know whether this will get rid of freckles, but running outside barefoot and taking the dew from the flowers to wash your face will sure wake you up!

SALVE FOR BURNS AND SKIN WOUNDS

We had a Balm of Gilead (or "Ban and Gilly Bud" as we kids called it) tree in our yard, and in the spring, we would make a salve by cooking the tender, young buds of this tree in butter or mutton tallow and Vaseline. This salve smells wonderful—like wintergreen!

HEADACHE REMEDY

We used to rub camphorated oil on our temples and forehead, or we would gather some fresh mint, crush it, make a poultice, and rest the poultice of crushed mint on the forehead. We used the mint that grew along the creeks, which we called "branch mint."

One of my favorite autumn stories is of Grandma Lindy Owens. She worked all the time trying to make a better home for her large family and her grandchildren. She took us with her when she hunted plants for her dyes. She taught us about the wild herbs for medicines and showed us where the spring greens grew. In the springtime, she would lead us through the woods and tell us about the plants and their uses and where the wildflowers grew.

A rare picture of Grandma Lindy. She spent most of her time working and singing old songs.

One late autumn day when the leaves had finally released their tenacious hold and were fluttering down one by one, Grandma decided to dye the family's winter clothes. Grandpap carried water and filled two black kettles. Then he built the fires for Grandma before riding his horse into town. In one kettle she had brown dye made from walnut hulls and in the other was blue dye made from indigo root.

On his way to town, Grandpap stopped by Mr. Sutton's house to see if he needed anything. He talked to the family for a while and was riding out of their yard when Mrs. Sutton asked, "Jim, what's Lindy doing today?" "She was dyeing when I left," Grandpap called back.

Mrs. Sutton grabbed her bonnet and tied it as she ran toward Grandma Lindy's house. All the way there she said she questioned the Lord about the worth of a heartless man like Jim, who would leave his wife dying. When Mrs. Sutton was almost in the yard, she heard Grandma Lindy singing and saw the boiling kettle. Grandma was stirring clothes around in the dye with her kettle stick as she sang. Then Mrs. Sutton realized what Grandpap had meant. The two women sat on the wash bench under the apple tree and laughed and laughed at themselves and Grandpap. Finally, Mrs. Sutton decided to dye her own bonnet and apron in the beautiful indigo blue while she and Grandma Lindy visited.

Our sweet baby twins Floyd and Freida.

The twins, Floyd and Freida did everything together as kids. Freida tells about the time they were put in different classes at school:

Being together was a natural thing, like breathing, and we never thought it would change—but it did when we started school. The first day was exciting and fun for us. We had new clothes. Floyd had a new green checked shirt and I had a green dress. We even had brand-new haircuts. My hair was cut in a Dutch girl bob and Floyd had a grown-up flat-top. Everything went well for the first few days. Then the teacher decided to separate us.

Now, I depended on Floyd and continued to do so at school those first few days. Floyd helped me color my pictures, do my homework, and he even told the teacher when I wanted to go to the restroom.

But one morning the teacher told Floyd he was moving into the classroom across the hall, and I would have to stay in the old classroom. I put up a big fuss, and it was the first time the teacher had seen me do anything on my own. I lost the argument, of course, and Floyd moved across the hall. He didn't want to leave me, because Mother had told us to take care of each other. I was crushed.

When I would look into Floyd's classroom and see all the fun things he was doing without me, tears would run down my cheeks. For the first time in my life I knew what it was like to be lonely.

Left to right: Randy, Rachel, and Floyd when they had a group called Southern Gallery.

The glasses came back to haunt Floyd again. They made school pictures the day he got his new glasses!

*W*henever we start talking about school, Floyd always reminds us of his ability to solve problems by telling this story:

Randy had girlfriends, Freida and Rachel had boyfriends—and I had eyeglasses! Each year a nurse from the health department would come to every school to check all the students' eyes to see whether we needed glasses. When I was in second grade, it was determined that I needed glasses. I didn't want glasses! I just knew they would ruin my life. Freida, my staunchest ally, was ready to help. After being fitted for the glasses, I decided that they were the cause of all my problems. In an attempt to rescue me from this horrible fate, Freida tried to wear them for me. But she couldn't see! She even tried to hide the glasses, but some meddling kid found them and returned them to us.

Together Freida and I conjured up a foolproof plan that would take care of my problems once and for all. After school, we buried my glasses under rocks and dirt in the road where the school buses ran. Sure enough, the next day someone found my bent and broken glasses. Randy and Rachel took them home to Mama. She couldn't fix them and she couldn't afford a new pair. I went through the rest of the school year, squint-eyed but happy.

When Papa and Mother were young, they were full of hopes and dreams. In November after their marriage, it was a certainty that Mother was pregnant and by June there would be a child. They both worked hard and enjoyed their home and life together, but Papa just couldn't give up his old life. He wanted the excitement he had been accustomed to before he married. On weekends, he would go on a spree with the boys and not bother to come home. At first he would be gone for just one night, but later he would stay gone all weekend.

Mother remembers how very afraid she was. The fear was a living, crawling thing that became her constant companion. She had never been alone before. She was used to the security of her big family. Now she was a prisoner of the dark, forbidding forest. She dreaded walking to the springhouse to get water because she had to go through the woods. She always tried to go in the middle of the day but sometimes she forgot, and she would have to go without water until it was daylight again.

The nights were a hell of darkness that Mother had to endure huddled alone in the bed she wanted to share with Papa. Whippoorwills would sit on the corners of the mud-daubed chimney and call to one another. Wild animals walked up to the porch and screamed defiantly at the house. To this day, Mother cannot bear being by herself. Even now she doesn't like to hear a whippoorwill because it reminds her of the nights she spent alone and frightened.

Mother sometimes reminisces and tells of the hard times and her early days with Papa. One Saturday, Mother told Papa how scared she was of being alone and begged him not to leave her there. But Papa had plans. She followed him to the back porch and leaned against the logs of the house. She was silent as she watched him shave and comb his hair. He had to stoop over to look into the broken piece of mirror fastened to the outside wall by nails bent over to hold it in place. She remained silent as he emptied the washpan into the yard and hung it up on a nail driven into the porch post. He dried his hands and threw the towel down beside the water bucket on the wooden shelf.

Mother picked up the damp towel and hung it up to dry on the wire clothesline that stretched between the porch posts. She turned to Papa and said, "Lee, you know I'm pregnant and it scares me to be up in this holler by

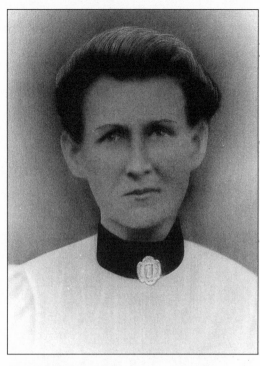

Albert Huston Parton.

Tennessee (Tenny) Parton.

George Washington and Cassie Ann Rayfield.

William Walter Parton.

Bessie Elizabeth Parton.

myself. Anything could happen." Papa just looked at her, then checked his appearance once more in the mirror. Mother walked over to him, took his arm, and turned him to face her. "If you leave me by myself tonight, I won't be here tomorrow. I'll go back home."

Papa pulled his arm loose from her hand and walked away. He was in a hurry. Mother didn't watch him leave. Instead she sat down on the steps and watched the chickens scratching around in the yard looking for bits of food.

She sat on the steps for a long time, trying to build her courage for what she knew she must do. At first she had been happy living there with Papa. She couldn't understand why he left her alone so much. In the three months they had lived together, she'd learned that Papa was stubborn, and, being a man, unpredictable. But Mother was stubborn, too, and a woman of her word even at sixteen years of age.

She swallowed her pride when she realized she would have to go back home and face all her people. She could just imagine their faces when they learned she had left Papa. Women didn't leave their husbands. They usually

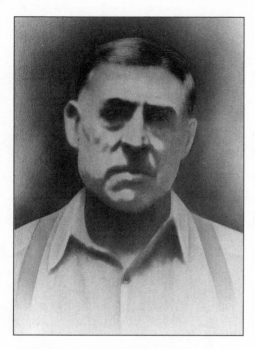
James Robert (Jim) Owens.

Mary Melinda (Lindy) Owens.

stayed, no matter how unhappy or how bad the situation. They just did the best they could.

Mother has always been stubborn. She makes a decision and never wavers. She decided that if Papa cared enough to change his ways, she would go back to him after a while, but she would teach him a lesson first. And if he didn't care for her enough to change, then she would try to close that chapter of her life.

She stood up and brushed off her dress. The moon was just beginning to peep over the top of the ridge and the darkness was slowly blanketing the hollow. The chickens had already flown up into the walnut tree to roost for the night. The chill of the wind was sharp as she went inside the cabin and locked the door. Mother put two more logs in the fireplace and warmed her hands as the flames curled around the fresh fuel. Mother's hands were trembling as she trimmed the wick of the oil lamp for the last time. There was just enough oil to last the night. The globe of the lamp was lined with soot, so she wiped it clean with a piece of brown paper. In the soft glow of the lamp she made a bundle of her clothes. There wasn't much to take—just a couple of dresses, a

Louisa Margaret Valentine.

Floyd Henry Valentine.

change of underclothes, and her Sunday shoes. The night was long and lonely and her only comforts were the glow of the lamp and the Bible she hugged to her breast. She slept fitfully.

The November frosts lay thick on the ground and on the webs of the field spiders, making them look like jewels on the dead grass and weeds. It had already frosted a few times, and the chill always lingered in the hollow until late in the day. It seemed as if the sun was in a hurry and wouldn't stay long in the hollow. There were always deep shadows, even at midday. The water in the branch had a thin edge of ice, and ice crystals had formed in the water bucket.

In the thin light of morning, Mother built a fire in the cookstove. She made biscuits and gravy and coffee. This would be her last meal in that house. She threw the leftover scraps out to the chickens and waited until the fire burned out in the stove. With one last look around, she put on her coat and tucked

The Reverend Jacob Robert (Jake) and Rena Kansas Owens.

Robert Lee Parton.

Avie Lee Carolina Parton.

the bundle of clothing under her arm. The cabin looked forlorn and empty as Mother quickly closed the door.

She hurried across the yard to the narrow sled road that led out of the hollow, and she never looked back once she began her journey. The sights and sounds of a late autumn were all around. Squirrels were busy gathering the last of the hickory nuts, acorns, and walnuts. Their busy chattering and running made Mother laugh. Sitting on a fallen tree, Mother watched the activity. All of a sudden it was quiet. The squirrels stopped and stood still; some quickly climbed trees. In the silence there was a slight rustling of laurel leaves. Mother became alert. Something was watching her, something that frightened the squirrels.

"Don't act scared. Walk slow, don't turn around," she kept telling herself. She didn't see anything, for whatever was there stayed at a distance, but she could hear the snapping twigs and the almost soundless brushing of leaves.

First it was on one side of her and then the other, always hidden by the dense undergrowth and laurel.

"Should I stand still or keep walking? Bobcats won't do anything, they just like to follow along out of sight. But what if it's a panther!" All the stories she had heard about panthers came rushing to her mind, adding to her sickening fear.

She began to think about all the worst stories she had heard, especially about panthers. Once a woman who lived in the mountains saw a panther reach through a window and snatch her tiny baby off the bed. She ran out to see the panther disappear into the laurel thickets carrying the baby in its mouth. Another woman took her toddler with her to hoe beans back in a hollow. A panther began stalking the child. The mother put the child behind her and fought the panther off with her hoe as she slowly walked backward out of the hollow. And not too long ago, a grown man had been nearly killed by a panther. He was walking through the woods when the panther jumped on his back. It dug the claws of its front feet into his shoulders and clawed his sheepskin coat to shreds with its hind feet. The man stabbed the panther with a knife until it turned him loose and ran off.

Mother desperately wanted to run. Her mind kept screaming, "Run, run!" but she forced her legs to plod along as if she had no fear. Gradually she walked faster and was relieved when she reached the end of the hollow. The rest of the trip was along the main road. Fortunately, her unknown follower didn't leave the dense shelter of the hollow to follow her across the open clearing.

She crossed the branch that ran clear and clean. The sun was hot now that she was out of the hollow and walking on the road. Mother removed her coat and wrapped it around the bundle of clothes she carried. She stopped to drink at the spring by the roadside. Her hands were still trembling as she took the tin can that was hanging on a limb. Such cans, called "community cups," were common in this area in the thirties and forties. The cans were usually rusty, but the people going by just rinsed them out, got a drink, and continued on their way.

Mother sat at the spring and rested for a while. She was tired, and she wished she could have stayed in her own home. But she shook her head as if to deny she had even thought about staying with Papa. It was over. She would forget.

Frisky came to meet her as she crossed the swinging bridge. The little shepherd walked along beside her until she started up the porch steps. She

Grandpa Jake Owens family in the 1930s. *Left to right:* Grandpa Jake, Prince, great-grandpap Jim, Jerry, Vonnie, great-grandma Lindy, Victor, great-aunt Dolly, Phillip, Lillie, and Annie.

opened the door and Grandma Rena looked at her in surprise. When she saw Mother's bundle of clothing she said nothing. Mother looked so little and tired, but her chin was stuck out in the familiar gesture of stubbornness.

Grandma Rena set another place at the table and then, after Mother had eaten, put her to bed. There would be time enough to talk after Mother was rested.

Being back home was difficult for Mother at first, having had a home of her own, but her family was good to her and their love for her was evident. Days stretched into weeks and Mother gradually settled into the familiar routine of living with her family again. She spent the time helping take care of her younger brothers and sister, waiting for the day when her own child would be born.

After waiting for what he considered enough time, Papa came to get Mother and take her back home with him. He figured he had let her suffer long enough and that she would be glad to go back with him after all this time. Besides, wives didn't leave their husbands!

Mother wouldn't go. She told him that he hadn't changed a bit and she wasn't going back to that awful place. She would just stay right there with her mama and daddy.

Papa left with his mind set; if that's the way she wanted it, then that's the way it would be. It probably wouldn't have worked out anyway, her being sixteen and so young and silly. He moved back into his parents' house.

May 24 was overcast and dreary. The cold spring rain had begun early in the afternoon. Grandpa Jake built a fire in the fireplace to take the damp chill from the house when Mother complained of being cold. Grandma Lindy, Uncle Sanberry, and Grandpap Valentine were there that day. They had come to see how Mother was doing.

Mother was restless and couldn't sit still, but she insisted she was all right. Grandma Rena had been watching her and knew better, so she sent Grandpa Jake and Uncle Sanberry to bring Dr. Thomas. The spring floods had washed away the swinging bridge, so Dr. Thomas came across the river in Uncle Sanberry's homemade boat.

The birth was uncomplicated and Mother says it was her easiest delivery. Grandma Lindy used to tell me that she was the first person to hold me and that I had more dark hair than any baby she had ever seen. All of Mother's babies had lots of hair when they were born, some dark like hers, some light like Papa's.

When word reached Papa that he was the father of a little girl, he brought a present, a little dress and a pair of baby shoes. Papa visited with his wife and child, but both Mother and Papa harbored resentment and nothing, not even the birth of their first child, could reestablish the bond.

Nearly a year passed before Papa came back to see us. He had grown a mustache and he seemed older and more determined. Papa had decided he didn't want anyone else raising his child. So he came back and talked to Mother again. He knew his responsibility, and he had been miserable not being able to take care of her and provide for his family. Being a Parton he felt this keenly, because above all else they love and provide for their children, and not doing his duty had made Papa sick with humiliation.

This time Mother was more willing to listen. She and Papa talked for a long time. No one knows what passed between them and I'm glad, for this was a private matter and deeply personal for both of them.

Their differences were settled. I was almost a year old, and there was a deep understanding between them that would last through all the difficult years they would face ahead.

I returned to the first home Mother and Papa had. The house was gone, but I took this picture of the walking trail Mother used when she went back home to her family.

Last November, Mother was making a pot of vegetable soup and she began talking about a teacher she remembers, Mayford Roberts. He impressed her as a child. He taught during the Depression, and he died as a young man, in his prime. He was a good but strict teacher. He cared about the children more than most, and he demanded the best from both boys and girls. He was married to Iva Ogle, Seldon Ogle's daughter. She came to school with him every day.

Iva helped him teach, and they taught grades one through eight. She would help the ones having a hard time with a subject or take care of a child who had come to school sick. The thing Mother remembered most was that Miss Iva put a big iron pot on the heater in the middle of the room and cooked a pot of soup for lunch. The older girls would help peel potatoes, onions, and turnips—whatever they had with them. Sometimes children would bring things from home for the soup.

Each child had a tin cup or bowl and spoon in the cloak room on a shelf. They each washed their own utensils at the water spout behind the school. Lots of children could only bring a piece of bread for lunch. It was wonderful to have a bowl of soup to dip the bread into. The older boys would wash the soup pot, dry it, and put it in the cloak room.

Mother knew that Seldon and Iva canned fresh vegetables every summer for soup during the cold months. Without those acts of kindness, many of those children would have gone for days without a nourishing meal.

Mother, Papa, and the kids. *Front row (left to right):* Cassie, Stella, Dolly (in front of Papa), Randy, Bobby, and Denver. *Back row:* David, Mother, Papa, and me.

$\mathcal{W}$e were gathered at Mother and Papa's house last September. Things had quieted down, and David's and Denver's children begged Mother and Papa to tell them something about their dads and their uncles, when they were growing up.

Papa said, "Well, girls, what I remember most about David and Denver was them working. I never saw anything like them. Now Bobby liked to do a little daydreaming now and then. Bobby and Floyd could always be found painting a picture or making pottery for your grandmother out of the sticky red clay that could be found in Sevier County."

Mother added, "They would spend hours making a vase or an ashtray or a plate. Bobby would also whittle animals and birds for gifts. Floyd always loved to plant, grow, cut, and arrange flowers. Even today we have shrubs and roses he planted as a child."

A "Dolly Day" parade in Sevierville.

My handsome son, Mitchell, and his beautiful wife, Kathy.

One cloudy day in the fall, my son, Mitchell, came over to my house to eat lunch. Mitchell is always trying to get us all in church and keep us there. He said, "Mom, when are you going to start church regular?"

I said, "Mitchell, you know I've been real busy."

He said, "Well, Mom, you're going to keep running around doing good for everybody until you *busy yourself* right out of your celestial home."

I finally told him, "Look, son, I'll probably be there serving angel cookies and ice cream before you ever get there!"

We both just laughed and went back to eating our lunch.

ecently Papa and I were sitting by the fire on a rainy day, and he recalled a sad story of his childhood:

The first thing I remember was the day my sister Margie was born. It was in the middle of the day, and Grandma Tenny was helping me build a play pigpen out of stovewood. I was playing like I was the pig and Grandma helped stack the wood high around me. The game Grandma Tenny and I were playing had gone on for some time when I heard a baby crying. I said, "There's a baby in our house." Grandma Tenny lifted me into her arms. "Lee, I believe you're right." She carried me inside to see my new baby sister.

My next vivid memories are of Margie's death eighteen months later, after having measles that turned into pneumonia. She died on a cold November night. Family and neighbors had been there with Mommy and Poppy and trying to help and give their support. Someone tolled the church bell once for the one year of her life. People used to do that, you know. The neighbors in the community came to our house all through the night. The women brought food and some of them cooked, while others sewed Margie's burial dress. The other women were busy sewing a padding, the lining for the coffin. Some just sat and tried to comfort Mommy. Two of my uncles made a little coffin of dark chestnut wood. It was Grandma Cass and Grandma Tenny who bathed my baby sister with camphor and dressed her for burial. When the body was ready and dressed in the clothes, the women laid her in the middle of my parents' feather bed. When the coffin was finished, the men tacked the soft lining the women had made inside. Grandma Cass took the tiny body from the bed and laid it in the coffin that sat on a table at the end of the bed.

Morning came. The men did the chores with Poppy and chopped a huge pile of wood; then they went home to do their own milking and feeding and to tend their stock. Several men took their picks and shovels to the graveyard and dug the grave.

Men carried the coffin half a mile to the church. A cold mist of rain was falling. Someone in black talked about God and things I didn't understand. The people sang hymns as they carried the coffin to the grave that had been dug in the churchyard. I remember the small mound of red clay behind the grave; it looked strange because the rain and mist made everything else look

Grandma Parton with her children. Papa is in the little shirt
dress in front.

gray. Someone took two ropes from a saddle and set the coffin on them. I had
wondered why they were getting ropes. The lid was nailed in place and then
the men lowered the coffin into the grave. Everyone was silent except for
Mommy's muffled sobs. Poppy was holding me in his arms, and I could feel
him crying, but he wasn't making a sound. My face was wet from the rain. I
looked around at Mommy and Poppy. Their faces were wet from the cold rain
and tears.

The men shoveled the red clay on top of the coffin and the wind blew fallen
leaves into the grave as they filled it up and mounded the dirt.

*W*hen my family gets together, our usual topic is each other. A recent gathering was no different. We laughed at ourselves and each other. But now, as we grow older, our children are our favorite targets.

Heidi

Randy was telling about Heidi when she was spending time with Mother and Papa. Heidi was about three or four at this time. Mother had gotten tired of babysitting, as she usually does, and had gone to bed. So Papa was watching out for Heidi while she played. Well, he wasn't doing a very good job of it, for she had managed to get his false teeth out of his shirt pocket.

She was playing on the floor, and he was half-asleep in his recliner, trying to keep an eye on her while she watched cartoons. She would talk to him and he would only grunt, half answering her.

Randy and Deb came to pick her up. She was leaning over the seat talking a mile a minute as they drove home. She patted Randy on the shoulder and said,

Rachel, Denver, and Cassie having a good time together.

Left to right: Freida, Stella, Cassie, Dolly, Rachel, and me. Looks like some of us got dressed for the wrong party!

"Dad, did you know Papaw can't see a thing or hear a word when he doesn't have his teeth in his mouth or pocket, one?" Randy had her repeat that story for days.

Randy went on to tell about the time Tever, his oldest daughter, was helping Papa work. She loved helping him work on the farm. This time when they picked her up, she wasn't happy and bubbly as usual. They had been making something for Dolly, and Mother, Papa, and Tever had worked very hard. Randy said, "What's the matter, Tever? You seem sad." She said, "Well, I am very sad. I just can't believe Aunt Granny (Dolly) works my Papaw so hard and he has to wear such ragged, awful-looking clothes."

Dolly at her theme park in Sevierville—Dollywood.

She has since learned these are Papa's favorite clothes, and even if Aunt Granny bought him suits, he wouldn't wear them. He prefers his old comfortable clothes.

Papa told a story about when Denver's daughter Jennifer used to help him carry wood. Even though she was tiny, she would grab up a big load. Papa would say something like, "Honey, that's too big a load for you. Don't carry so much." And Jennifer would reply, "Oh, Papaw, I'm strong and I was born tough."

A Sunday afternoon family gathering. We are on Mother and Papa's back porch. Bryan, the shortest boy, is teasing Clint.

Then Papa told about the time Cassie's three-year-old son Bryan was riding to the store with him and they almost got hit. Papa threw on the brakes, and Bryan fell out of the seat (we didn't have to wear seatbelts then). While Papa was cursing the driver of the other car, Bryan jumped up and brushed off his clothes. Then he drew back his little fist at Papa. He thought Papa was fussing at him. Papa stopped the truck and explained to Bryan that he wasn't mad at him. He was angry at the driver of the other car. Bryan and Papa are a lot alike, and Bryan still has that quick temper, just like his grandfather.

Mother started telling tales on the granddaughters. She laughed about Dena's way of saying she had a bright idea. She would tell Mother that she had a big thunderstorm, instead of a brainstorm. Jada said for a long time that when she would get aggravated, she would just do what Mama Deene does. Once Mother asked her, "Just what it is that Mama Deene does." She said, "Oh, you know, she just keeps on going like the Energizer Bunny."

Papa talked about the time Bobby fell out of the car and bounced like a ball on the pavement, then rolled over a couple of times. By the time Papa got the car stopped, Bobby was running toward him, carrying his little railroad cap in his hand, brushing off his new overalls. Papa asked him if he was hurt. He said, "No, but I got my overalls dirty." He was skinned but otherwise unhurt. Papa picked him up in his arms and carried him, checking his limbs, but none were broken. Papa said they sat there by the side of the road for some time, because he was so shaken he couldn't drive.

That was the same black Studebaker that I had almost fallen out of. The door was messed up. After taking the latch off and wiring the door closed, so no one else would get hurt, Papa finally sold the car. Later we asked Papa if he had been trying to get rid of us. He told us no and added, "I was already rid of Willadeene. She was married, and Bobby was just about the best kid I had. So I didn't want to get rid of him for sure."

Winter

A white stillness is upon the earth.
The trees are naked and cold
underneath the white, cold blanket.
The ground is hard, dark and spewing,
as if fighting back.
The gray clouds hover close
as if trying to warm
the shivering earth,
but they're cold, too.
A rabbit runs
with snow flying in the air behind him,
looking for food.
The dog chases the rabbit
for the same purpose.
We come inside from
cutting piles of wood
and make the fire hotter.
Then we eat and drink
and we laugh
on a winter evening.

$\mathcal{N}$ow there was only so much one could do for entertainment on long winter evenings when our young bodies were tired and our nerves thin. We didn't have TV. We didn't even have electricity. We couldn't go to drive-in movies. We didn't even have a car until after Randy was born. So Mother and Papa fought! No blows were struck—it was a battle of voicing their opinions. Now this fight happened once or twice a year. It didn't stop until Mother

Mother, Papa, and Stella at one of Stella's shows. Cousin Dwight Puckett is on drums.

announced that she was
going to leave Papa, and that
meant we were involved, too.
Who wanted to go with
Mother? Who wanted to stay
with Papa? We'd look around
at our safe, warm house
where food, security, and all
the familiar things were. It
was a hard choice to make.
Papa was staying. Mother
was going.

I can still see Papa sitting
in his chair saying, "Damn it
to hell, Avie Lee! You're
upsettin' the kids!"

David always stood by
Papa. He was smart. He
wasn't about to go anywhere.

Left to right: Denver, David, Papa, and Floyd. The house
was built by Mother and Papa in 1956.

Denver and I couldn't bear the thought of Mother going away and leaving us,
probably forever, so we always stood by her. When Bobby, Stella, and Cassie
were little, we would make their decision for them. Denver and I would stand
there holding them on Mother's side of the room.

Dolly couldn't be disloyal to either parent. She would be so undecided that
she'd run to Mother, but then when she'd look over at Papa, she'd run to him.
This would go on for a while. The more she would run back and forth, the
funnier she got. Finally, Mother and Papa would get tickled, and the big fight
would be over. But we kids would still be upset.

After the fight was over, Denver and I would be mad at David, because he
would have had everything by staying with Papa. We would have been
destitute and had nothing but Mother. No food, no home. David would play
by himself, building roads and tunnels in the dirt behind the house, and
running his little wooden cars and wagons that he made himself. We would
try to make him lonely by not playing with him. But, he would do such fun
things that we never let him suffer very long. Now that I think about it, he was
probably happy when we left him alone for a while.

*E*very winter wood was cut and dragged into the wood yard to be cut up with a crosscut saw. Papa liked hickory and oak because they are hardwoods. They burn with more heat and last longer; and most important, they don't pop and throw sparks like some other wood does. We'd work along with him and we knew well how to use the crosscut saw, boys and girls alike. After some of the wood was sawed up in one-and-a-half-foot lengths, Papa and the boys would split it up into stovewood and stack it in the woodshed. We'd have to carry in stovewood every evening for Mother to burn in the cookstove. We would pile it down on the floor by the stove.

One of my very favorite pictures of Dolly. We all love our pets.

There was a big stack of logs outside near the house. It would last for a while, but we had to cut wood whenever we could, for the winters were long and Papa wanted to be sure there would always be enough wood to keep us warm.

I think everything we learned as children was good, and even necessary in our lives now. A couple of years ago, a severe ice-and-snow storm left us without electricity for days. I still live much the same way we did growing up. I built a fire in the wood cookstove that once belonged to my parents and made the fire hotter in the fireplace. Lots of friends and relatives ended up at my house. My older brothers and I could show the younger ones how to cut the wood to fit the fireplace and the cookstove. We ended up having a wonderful time.

$\mathcal{W}$e loved to do things outside in the winter, especially play in the snow. One winter morning, when I was about ten years old, we got up and looked out and the world was a fairyland of white. The mountains looked as if they had been draped with a white satin sheet that fell in folds. Everywhere the trees were hanging heavy with snow. The spruce trees were laden, their limbs bowed low to the ground. Red birds and blue jays surprised us with flashes of bright crimson and blue against the snow. The hollow was quiet. Even the sounds of the children playing outside were muffled by the snow.

The white smoothness was broken by the tracks of dogs, cats, and tiny wild animals that had crept quietly across the snow during the night. A rabbit kicked up a spray of snow in the air behind him as Brownie gave chase, hoping for a tasty rabbit dinner. The two ran the length of the field. They zigzagged back and forth and then ran the length of it again. The rabbit, tired of the chase, disappeared into the woods, and Brownie, not so sure he really wanted rabbit, trotted back to the house.

The boys built a snow house. They worked all day packing the snow and piling it high for the walls. When they finished the walls, leaving a hole for the door, they placed a piece

Our brother David at Christmas when we were growing up.

Randy posing just like David did.

Bobby in the army.

of tin over the top for the roof and then packed snow on top of that. It was a house the Eskimos would have envied—but off limits to the girls! It was like the boys' club or hunting lodge. We decided that if we couldn't go inside, at least we could get on top of it. So we sneaked up, one by one, to the back of the snow house.

Dolly and I had just stepped onto the roof when it all caved in. The boys were inside the snow house. I didn't know boys could scream; they sounded just like us girls! Brownie came running. We must have been a sight. The girls were digging, Brownie was digging, and, of course, the boys were digging. When we finally got them out, I asked, "David, what in the world happened? I heard a rumble and then you'uns screamed. So we ran out here and the snow

Denver as a teenager. I wonder whether he is remembering the snow house or maybe the time he left David in town with the ugly girls.

house was gone. We thought you had all been killed!"

Now sometimes it was better (at least where the boys were concerned) not to confess to anything. We'd learned that the hard way. They hadn't seen us on the roof of the snow house and just thought we came to help after the roof collapsed. All David could remember was how everything shook, then the snow-covered roof came down. The boys were confused, and after discussing it among themselves, they concluded that they had survived a great earthquake. And with each telling of it, it got worse, until they were convinced that so great was the earthquake that the mountains had shifted and the house moved downhill at least three feet. They couldn't believe that Mother and Papa hadn't felt the huge tremor. And then they remembered that the Bible said that in the last days there would be earthquakes. Oh, Lord! We were in the last days! For two full days after that, we girls could get by with anything and not have to worry about the boys' fists. They were so good to us. But when the world went on and the end of time was slow in arriving, the boys forgot their fears and life was back to normal.

inter shadows fall early in the mountains. I remember the warm, secure feeling of winter evenings. The cellar underneath the house was full. The walls were lined with plank shelves eight inches wide and one inch thick. On these shelves were home-canned vegetables, meat, fruit, pickles, and relishes. On the well-swept, hard-packed dirt floor sat large crocks of pickled beans and corn, crocks of kraut, crocks of pickled corn on the cob, and a crock of chowchow (pickled relish) to eat with meat and potatoes and dried beans. There were other crocks of Papa's homemade wine, cider, pumpkinjack, and applejack. There was a jar of moonshine for medicinal purposes—and Papa's personal pleasure.

The old black kettle was the most important item in the household. Like a lot of other families, we continued to use ours through the 1960s. We heated water in it to wash and dye clothes, and we made lye soap in it. We rendered

Mother's trusty old iron kettle.

lard in it when we killed hogs. We used the kettle to make hominy and sometimes to cook stew.

Out in the back yard we had a special "tater hole," or root cellar, where Papa put the potatoes. He always picked out two bushels of good ones to plant the next spring and put these to one side. The tater hole was just a big hole in the ground with straw on its floor and sides, and the potatoes and turnips were poured into it and covered with more straw. Then the wooden door was closed and dirt thrown on top. You could walk right by without seeing it if you didn't know it was there. When we needed potatoes, we'd take a bushel basket and fill it up so we'd have enough for several days.

The walls of the kitchen were full of nails where dried fruit, peppers, garlic, dill, onions, and dried beans (shuck beans) were hung. We grew our own dill, garlic, and asparagus behind the woodshed. We also grew red and black raspberries behind the smokehouse, where we kept the salted pork, as well as a variety of other things. Cardboard boxes filled with dried shellie beans, corn, crowder and black-eyed peas, and dried apples were stacked by the cupboard.

There were two sacks full of walnuts, hazelnuts, hickory nuts, chinquapins, and beechnuts. We'd sit in front of the fireplace and put the handle of a flatiron between our knees with the smooth surface up, crack nuts on it with a hammer, and throw the hulls into the fire. Walnuts were cracked to use in fudge

Mother holding on to her Dolly.

or just to eat with salt. We always had to crack some extra ones for the smaller children.

A kettle full of simmering soup, pinto beans, or dried peas with ham usually hung over the open fireplace, and the Dutch oven would be warming on the hearth for corn bread and sometimes crackling bread.

When supper was over, Papa would take his tobacco out of his pocket and either roll a cigarette or fill his pipe. Long shadows were cast on the wall from the soft glow of the oil lamp. Mother and Papa sat and talked in the evening, and it seemed they always had a lot to talk about. We tried to hear every word they said, and we liked to watch the strange, funny shadows of their profiles on the walls.

Eventually Papa would push back his chair, often lifting a child or two from his lap, and take what scraps and cornbread were left from supper out to the dogs. The girls stacked up the dishes and wiped down the oilcloth on the table. While we washed the dishes in pans on the wood cookstove, Mother put the little ones to bed and Papa fastened the night latch. Sometimes Mother and Papa would put new bottoms in chairs at night. They both knew how to repair cane- and twine-bottom chairs.

We were all glad when it snowed because then we could have snow cream! Mother would make peach, apple, or blackberry cobbler and Papa would go outside and scoop up a pan full of fresh, fluffy snow. Dolly always grabbed the big wooden spoon so she would have the important job of stirring the snow cream as the rest of us added milk, sugar, and vanilla flavoring. I think she hid the spoon so none of us could find it and get to stir the snow cream. We'd try to take the spoon away from her, and we'd get our knuckles cracked with the spoon for our efforts. I don't think anyone ever got that spoon away from her.

Dolly and Skip Trotter, from WSEV radio station, which is now WDLY, Dolly's station in Sevierville.

The kitchen was our favorite room, especially during the colder months, and we were always underfoot trying to see what Mother was cooking. When we built our new house, the one I live in now, the kitchen was big and roomy. The table Papa made sat in the middle of the room. A cane bottom chair was placed at each end of the table, and on either side were long benches for the children. The kerosene lamp sat in the middle of the red-and-white checkered oilcloth on the table. The wood cookstove had a reservoir on the side for heating water and a warmer on top to heat leftovers. Along the wall next to the stove was a low table two-and-a-half-feet wide by five feet long. This was called the side table or water table.

    Mother sewed an elastic band on pretty colored sweet-feed sacks and made a skirt for the side of the table that hid all the lard cans, boxes of canned food, and pots and pans we stored under the table. She tacked the band of the skirt along the edge of the table. It brightened the room and matched the curtains. We loved the sweet-feed sacks and couldn't wait for them to become empty. The hundred-pound sacks were made of pretty cotton material. Some had flowers and feminine designs, and some had tiny dogs or horses on them.

Sweet feed, as we called it, was made from bran, molasses, and grain. This was fed to the cows when we milked. We'd dump about a quart of sweet feed in the feed box, along with nubbins (small ears of corn that grow on the top of the cornstalks). The feed box was about two feet square, made from rough planks. The sides were a foot high. We had one nailed to the wall next to the gear room in the barn shed. There were depressions worn in the bottom of the feed box where the cows had licked the sweet bran over the years. We had hens that liked to lay their eggs in the feed box, so we had to check the box before milking time.

There were small feed boxes in the stables the hens must have thought were nests, too. Each stable had a manger where we threw the hay from the loft for the horse and cows. The cows ate the shuck, corn, and cob, but the horse's corn had to be shucked because he ate only the kernels. So did the pigs. If we threw unshucked ears of corn to the pigs, they'd shuffle them around in the mud and eat some, but most of it would be wasted. So we always had to shuck it.

There was also a meal bin in the kitchen, a big chest with a lid. It had two sections inside, one for meal and one for flour. The only other piece of furniture in the kitchen was a white cabinet. It had a pull-out shelf trimmed in red that was like a countertop made of porcelain. We used it to roll out biscuit dough. We kept what few bowls, plates, and cups we had in the top section, along with the pint jars, pie pans, and bucket lids. We kept our forks, knives, and spoons—none of which matched—in the wide drawer under the shelf.

The kitchen seemed to be the busiest room in the house. We would fix the younger children a playhouse under the big kitchen table so they wouldn't be underfoot. The older children would sit on the bench behind the table and read or try their hand at songwriting. Some just sat with their elbows on the table and chins propped in their hands, watching what everyone else was doing.

We practiced table manners eating from pie pans and bucket lids that we used for plates, and drinking from snuff glasses and pint Mason jars. Dishes didn't last long at our house. They were broken by the little ones by accident or by the older children doing the dishes when they wanted to be doing something else.

In our minds we explored the world and its riches. We also plumbed the depths of nature, and our inner selves. We questioned the rules of society and wondered who decided what was right and proper and tasteful. We watched people who were considered to be important people in the community and found they were no different and no better than we were. They just wore expensive clothes and lived in finer homes, but we were never envious of them. To tell the truth, we thought we had everything we needed. We still have many of these plates and glasses, and we enjoy using them to this day.

Papa and Dolly going somewhere on Dolly's bus.

Even with all the work of taking care of children and doing enormous loads of washing by hand, Mother still took the time to use her imagination and ingenuity to create recipes that we all learned and still use today. If someone told Mother how to cook something, she would take note of a few of the basic ingredients and go into the kitchen and create her own recipe. Her revised recipes were more to her satisfaction and ours.

Mother added wonder to our lives as we watched the magic of her stone soup unfold. She would take a clean white stone, put it in a pot of water, and then explain to the kids about the man who went to an old woman's house and asked for something to eat. The old woman told him she didn't have any food, so he asked her to get a pot of water. Then he took a stone and put it into the water and kept telling her they needed just a little bit of this and a bit of that for the soup. We were enthralled by the story and just as surprised as the old woman in the story when we saw that the stone had made this wonderful soup.

When Mother was in a really good mood, she would make gingerbread men and give the smaller children the very important job of holding the oven door shut so the gingerbread men couldn't get out and run away. Mother was always using what we call "food extenders," ingredients that would make a bigger batch out of just a little bit. She'd use fat raw meat skins to grease the bread pans; it didn't waste lard. She added water to catsup and mustard. They were thin but they lasted a long time. By the time the jars were empty you could almost see through the mustard and catsup. If we had just a few fish, Mother would fry "dry-land fish." This was cornmeal mush fried in the same grease she fried the fish in. It tasted like the fish, but without

An Easter Sunday picture. *Front row (left to right):* Denver, Floyd, and Randy. *Back row (left to right):* Papa, Mother, David, and Bobby.

the bones! We had ham omelets before we knew what they were called, because it was a way for the whole family to have ham and eggs without using a whole ham for one meal.

Sometimes Mother would tell us a story to make the meal more interesting. She could make very ordinary food seem magic to us. Mother used to make baked beans she called "cowboy beans." Young cowboys in our family ate them without complaining because they were made especially for them. A dish of fried potatoes, onions, and sweet peppers was for the Indian braves. Mother couldn't feed just the cowboys

Of course, Dolly always had to eat some of the Indians' food and the cowboys' food!

and let the Indians starve! She makes a delicious salmon stew, and her chili can't be compared to any I've eaten. Chocolate cake (baked in an iron skillet) with hot chocolate syrup or fudge frosting poured over it, banana pudding with meringue, chicken and dumplings, potato soup, potato cakes, bread pudding—I could go on and on, but this makes me so hungry.

Mother used all her imagination to cook dishes that we'd like; otherwise the meals would have been boring, because our basic ingredients for almost every meal were beans, potatoes, meal, flour, lard along with eggs, pork, chicken, or some wild game.

We canned food and preserved it all year long. In the winter we made jelly from the juices Mother had canned in the summer. On cold winter days the house might smell of peach, plum, or more often, blackberry juice being boiled down to jelly. The jelly was always made in an enamel-coated dishpan or cooker. We skimmed the foam off with a big spoon or the water dipper and put it into a white ironstone bowl to cool for breakfast the next morning, to have with butter and hot biscuits. Sometimes we couldn't wait so we'd have the jelly, butter, and biscuits for supper. We canned fresh pork after Thanksgiving and made sausage and canned it. We sulphured apples on the back porch in a crock. The sulphur was lit in the bottom of the crock and covered with a tin can with holes in it. The crock was filled with freshly peeled apples; then it was covered with a clean white cloth. The sulphur burned slowly, with the smoke going through the apples to preserve them. They were a light cream color after smoking. We washed the apples when we wanted to eat them just out of the crock or to make fried pies. We called the sulphured apples "smoked fruit."

Nothing was wasted. The first cress, or "cressy greens" as we called them, and poke sallit greens were canned. These were things we hated to smell cooking, because the odor was so strong it was almost toxic! It was great when they were almost done, because then they were rinsed off and bacon grease was added. Then they smelled good.

When Mother was in bed with a new baby, Papa did the cooking, which was all right for a day or two. He would tell us he made left-handed gravy and biscuits, that his cooking would make us pretty or smart, make us left-handed like him, or whatever he thought up. No matter what he said, the little ones would stand at Mother's bed and eat off her plate. She would feed them as they told her how they wished she'd get well because they didn't like Papa's left-handed cooking. But Papa and Grandma wouldn't let Mother get out of bed for nine days. And when she was able to cook for us again, we sure appreciated it.

$\mathcal{M}$other and I sat down one afternoon and put together some of our family's favorite recipes. These are written just as Mother used them. Most of these recipes will feed a large family. However, they can be cut down and tailored for any number of people.

Try at your own risk! We hope you enjoy them.

Dandelion Greens

Wash two or three handfuls of dandelion greens in several waters (until free from dirt and insects). If tender, place moist greens in a kettle without water. Cover tightly and cook 6 minutes. If old, place them in 1/2 to 1 cup of boiling water, cover tightly, and boil until tender. Drain. Push through a colander or chop until fine. Season with salt, pepper, and butter. Serve garnished with slices of hard-cooked eggs.

Wilted Lettuce

1 large bowl leaf lettuce, cut up
4 to 6 green onions, cut up, blades and all
1/4 cup vinegar
6 to 8 slices bacon

Toss the lettuce with the onions and vinegar. Fry the bacon and pour the hot bacon grease onto the salad. Sprinkle bits of bacon over the top of salad, if you wish. Toss and serve at once.

Biscuits

2 cups unsifted, self-rising flour
1/2 cup shortening
3/4 cup milk or buttermilk

Place the flour in a bowl; cut in the shortening with a pastry blender or a fork. Add the milk all at once and mix lightly. Turn out dough onto a floured surface; knead lightly. Pat down to about 1/2-inch thickness. Cut out the biscuits with a floured glass or biscuit cutter. Place on a baking sheet. Bake at 400° for 12 to 15 minutes or until done. Makes 12 to 14 biscuits.

Fried Corn Bread

1 cup cornmeal
1/4 cup flour
1 teaspoon sugar
1 egg
1/2 cup milk or buttermilk
1 very small onion, finely cut (optional)
1 tablespoon cooking oil or bacon grease
Cooking oil or bacon grease to fry, about 4 tablespoons.

Combine the cornmeal, flour, sugar, egg, milk, onion, and oil. Warm the remaining oil in a skillet and fry spoonfuls of batter until brown on both sides. Makes 8 small or 4 large fritters.

Stewed Chicken and Dumplings

Wash a skinless chicken and cut it into serving pieces. Drop the chicken into boiling water that has one small carrot (chopped), one small onion (chopped), two cloves of garlic (sliced), and salt already added. Add water to cover the chicken by 2 or 3 inches. Cover the pot and simmer for about 2 hours. Remove the chicken from the pot. Drop dumplings (see recipe below) in the simmering liquid. Meanwhile, remove the chicken meat from the bone and gently place it back into the pot. Add 2 tablespoons of butter and 1/4 teaspoon black pepper. Don't stir. Cover and let simmer for 15 minutes or until dumplings are tender and fluffy inside.

Dumplings

1 cup flour
2 tablespoons baking powder
1/4 teaspoon salt
1 egg
1/2 cup whole milk

Sift the flour with the baking powder and salt. Mix the egg with the milk and add all at once to the dry ingredients. Stir only until mixed. Drop by spoonfuls into boiling chicken broth. Cover and simmer for 15 minutes before removing the lid. Serve immediately.

Note: If you decide to use self-rising flour, omit the baking powder.

Oysters Fried

These are some updated versions of Mother's oyster recipes.
She used to use canned oysters and green tops of onions instead of fresh oysters,
parsley, and celery.

Wash and drain 1/2 pint fresh oysters. Season with salt and pepper. Roll the oysters in flour, dip them in beaten egg, and then roll them in cracker or bread crumbs. Roll off any surplus crumbs. Press each oyster flat into its original shape and drop into hot deep fat. Fry to a golden brown, drain well, and garnish with lemon and parsley. Serve with crackers, celery, or cole slaw, and catsup.

Oyster Stew

1/4 cup butter
1 pint oysters, with liquid
1 1/2 cups milk
1/2 cup cream
1/2 teaspoon salt
1/8 teaspoon pepper
2 tablespoons chopped parsley

Melt the butter in the top of a double boiler and add the oysters. Bring to the boiling point but do not boil. Pour the milk and cream over the hot oysters. When the oysters come to the surface, add salt, pepper, and chopped parsley. Serve immediately.

Mother's Chili

1/2 gallon white navy beans, cooked according to package directions
1 pound ground beef or pork, fried but not browned
2 cups catsup
2 cups strong coffee
Salt and pepper to taste
Dash cayenne pepper
Enough chili powder to make it as "hot" as you like it
 (we used 1 teaspoon)

Simmer all the ingredients for 45 minutes to 1 hour.

Cowboy Beans

1 pound ground beef
2 medium onions, chopped fine
1 small bell pepper, chopped fine
1 large can pork and beans or 1 quart cooked October beans
2 cups catsup
1 teaspoon vinegar
3 teaspoons brown sugar or 1 cup Karo syrup
2 teaspoons mustard
1 teaspoon salt
1 teaspoon pepper

Brown the ground beef, onions, and pepper. Add the remaining ingredients.
Pour into a baking dish and bake at 300° for about 15 minutes.

Corn Cut from the Cob

Cooked corn may be cut from the cob and reheated with cream and butter. Or cut raw corn away from the cob and cook it in its own juices with a little water. Fresh corn also can be placed in a saucepan or skillet with hot melted butter or a small amount of bacon grease, and cooked until tender. Good with fried corn bread and tomato and onion slices.

Lemon Pie

1/4 cup cornstarch
1 cup sugar
1/8 teaspoon salt
1 cup boiling water
1 tablespoon butter
2 eggs, separated (yolks beaten; whites beaten to stiff peaks
  with 2 tablespoons powdered sugar)
1 lemon rind, grated (from 1 large lemon)
1/4 cup lemon juice (from about 2 lemons)
1 prebaked pie crust

In a saucepan, mix the cornstarch, sugar, and salt. Add the water slowly, stirring to dissolve all of the ingredients. Cook over medium heat for 5 minutes, stirring constantly. Add the butter, remove from heat and cool slightly. Add the beaten egg yolks, lemon rind, and lemon juice; mix well. Pour the filling into the baked pie shell and top with the beaten egg whites. Brown in a slow oven (300° to 325°).

Pumpkin Pie

2 cups canned pumpkin
1/2 cup sugar
1/4 teaspoon nutmeg
1/2 teaspoon cinnamon
1/2 teaspoon ginger
1/4 teaspoon salt
1 cup milk
1 egg, beaten
1 pie shell (baked for 5 to 10 minutes at 400° to 425°)

Mix the pumpkin with the sugar, spices, salt, and milk, and heat through. Stir in the egg and pour the mixture into the baked pie shell. Bake for 25 to 45 minutes in a moderate (350° to 375°) oven until done.

Angel Cookies

2 egg whites
1 teaspoon each vinegar and vanilla extract
2 cups powdered sugar, sifted
2 cups chopped pecans

Beat the egg whites until stiff. Add the vinegar and vanilla. Gradually add the powdered sugar. Fold in the pecans. Drop by teaspoonfuls onto a greased cookie sheet. Bake for 10 to 12 minutes at 300°.

Hello Dolly Cookies

1/4 cup shortening
1/4 cup margarine or butter
1/2 teaspoon cinnamon
1/2 teaspoon nutmeg
1 cup all-purpose flour
1/2 cup granulated sugar
1/4 cup packed brown sugar
1 egg
1 teaspoon vanilla extract
1/8 teaspoon baking soda

In a mixing bowl beat the shortening and margarine or butter with an electric mixer on medium to high speed for 30 seconds. Add the cinnamon and nutmeg to the flour. Add about half of the flour to the butter mixture along with the sugar, brown sugar, egg, vanilla, and baking soda. Beat until thoroughly combined. Beat in the remaining flour. Drop by rounded teaspoons 2 inches apart onto an ungreased cookie sheet. Bake at 375° for 8 to 10 minutes or until the edges are golden. Cool the cookies on the cookie sheet for 1 minute, then remove and cool on a wire rack. Makes about 24 cookies.

Dolly at Dollywood.

Banana Pudding

1 large box vanilla wafers
1 1/2 pounds bananas, sliced
1/2 cup sugar
1/4 cup flour
3 large eggs, separated
1/4 cup butter
Dash salt
3 cups whole milk
1 teaspoon vanilla extract

Place the sliced bananas and vanilla wafers in a large pan. In a large heavy saucepan (or preferably the top of a double boiler), mix together the sugar, flour, egg yolks, butter, and salt. Add the milk, a little at a time, while stirring. Cook slowly stirring constantly until the mixture thickens. Let it cool for a few minutes, then add the vanilla. Pour over the bananas and vanilla wafers. Top with meringue (see below).

Meringue Topping

3 egg whites
1/2 teaspoon sugar
1/2 teaspoon lemon juice
1/2 teaspoon vanilla extract

Beat the 3 egg whites with the sugar, lemon juice, and vanilla until stiff. Spoon this mixture over the top of the pudding and brown in the oven at 475°.

Quick Yellow Cake

1/2 cup soft butter
1 cup sugar
2 eggs
1/2 cup milk
1 3/4 cups cake flour, sifted
1/2 teaspoon salt
2 1/2 teaspoons baking powder
1 teaspoon vanilla extract

Sift the dry ingredients. Combine with the other ingredients in a bowl and beat well for 2 or 3 minutes using a wire whisk or rotary beater. Bake the cake in a greased 9x12-inch pan or in two 8 1/2-inch layer pans in a moderate oven (350° to 375°) for 12 to 25 minutes. Frost as desired.

Variations:
Quick Chocolate Cake: Substitute 1/4 cup cocoa for 1/4 cup flour.
Quick Caramel Cake: Substitute 1 1/4 cups packed brown sugar for the white sugar. Bake in a 9x12-inch pan. Ice with uncooked white icing. Decorate with evenly spaced pecan halves. Cut cake so that a nut meat will be in the center of each square or bar.

Gingerbread
(or Sweet Bread)

1/2 cup sugar
1/2 cup butter
1 cup molasses
2 cups flour
1 1/2 teaspoon powdered ginger
1/2 teaspoon baking soda
1/2 teaspoon cinnamon
1/2 cup buttermilk

Combine all ingredients and mix well. Bake at 350° in a bread pan for about 1 hour or until done. Decorate with powdered sugar or icing if desired.

Jam Cake

1/2 cup butter
1 cup sugar
3 egg yolks
1 cup jam
2 cups sifted flour
1/2 teaspoon cinnamon
1/2 teaspoon nutmeg
1 teaspoon soda
1/4 cup sour cream
3 egg whites, beaten

Cream the butter and sugar and beat in the egg yolks. Stir in the jam. Resift the flour with the other dry ingredients. Add the flour mixture to the butter and sugar in about three parts, alternating with the sour cream. Beat the batter after each addition until well blended. Fold in beaten egg whites. Bake in two greased 9-inch layer pans or in a 9-inch tube pan in a moderate (325° to 350°) oven for 25 to 50 minutes. Frost as desired.

Caramel Frosting

2 cups brown sugar
1 cup milk or cream
3 tablespoons butter
1 teaspoon vanilla extract

Slowly boil the sugar and milk or cream to the soft ball stage (238°). Add the butter, remove from the heat, and cool. Add the vanilla and beat until thick and creamy. If it is too heavy, thin the icing with a little hot cream until it is the right consistency for spreading.

$\mathcal{M}$other did a lot of sewing, especially during the winter months. She used her old treadle Singer sewing machine to make new clothes, to patch old clothes, and to alter hand-me-downs. She could take a few packs of Rit clothes dye, a day of hard work, and we'd have a new outfit. Of course, we didn't have many because, remember, there were eleven of us to clothe.

Our pillowcases and sheets were made from the white coarse cloth of hundred-pound feed and fertilizer sacks that we bleached by boiling them in lye water in the wash kettles. We used a long stick to keep the sacks pushed under the water, but a few stains of the red and blue lettering still showed faintly if we girls bleached them. We'd forget to keep them pushed under the water or we'd wander off to play with our brothers, whose job it was to keep the fire going. After the sacks were bleached, they were washed several times to soften them.

Sheets made from these sacks were almost impossible to wear out. They remained rough and scratchy no matter how many times they were washed. The seams felt like two-by-fours if you had to sleep on one.

We were taught early on to "waste not, want not." Not only were we taught it, we also lived it faithfully. Worn-out clothes, such as overalls and wool shirts, were never thrown away. They were cut into squares and sewn together for quilts. The worn-out quilts were used for the batting inside the new ones. Mother very seldom quilted them because it took so long. Instead, she tacked them together with yarn or heavy cotton thread. Our potholders were denim squares cut out of worn-out overalls and sewn several layers thick on the sewing machine. Our towels and washcloths were made out of feed and fertilizer sacks.

We embroidered pretty flowers on our towels and pillowcases so they wouldn't look so plain. Our dishtowels and table scarves were made from the softer and more finely woven flour sacks and we always embroidered them. We had the type of embroidery patterns that were transferred to the material by pinning the paper pattern to the cloth and running a hot iron over the paper. If we were careful, we could use the same pattern again. When the ink wouldn't leave the pattern on cloth anymore, we'd use carbon paper and trace the pattern onto our cloth.

We made homemade starch from plain flour and water. Later we had Faultless starch. After starching and when the clothes were dry, we had to sprinkle them by dipping our hands in water and flipping it on the clothes. Then we packed the dampened clothes in a pillowcase until they were ready to iron.

The boys always had to have their jeans starched extra stiff and the sharp crease in the legs had to be ironed until it would last and last. David always ironed his own jeans, because no one else could do it to suit him. But Denver just wanted his ironed any old way, and he'd try to hire one of the girls to do it for him. When he was desperate, he'd even let one of the littler ones iron his jeans, because Denver was the marble champion in our family and he had better things to do.

Sevier County Police Department escorting Dolly to a show in the late 1970s.

*T*he winter before Dolly was born, Mother, David, Denver, and I were sick with the flu. Within a few days, Denver and I were getting better and enjoying all the attention of Papa taking care of us.

Mother was worse and not able to get out of the bed. We were all worried about David, too, because he coughed constantly and his fever wouldn't go down. Papa asked Mother if she could manage us while he went to get Grandma Rena to send Uncle Wesley for Dr. Thomas. When Papa left he said, "Willadeene, take care of them for me while I'm gone." He put David in the bed with Mother, and I sat in a straight-backed chair pushed against her bed, holding Denver in my lap. We sat and waited for what seemed like hours. The fire was dying down in the fireplace. I put Denver in the bed beside David and said, "Mother, it's cold in here. I'm going to the kitchen and get some stovewood and put it on the fire. I can't lift the logs."

I carried an armload, which, for me, was four sticks of wood. Mother rose up on her elbow and said, "Just lay them on top of the coals. Don't throw them, Willadeene. Be careful."

Mother and Papa never quarreled at us for trying to do the necessary things. I guess that is why we older ones grew up knowing how to do grown-up work. But I was only a little girl, and when I had carried three armloads of wood and put them on the fire, I was still enough of a baby to want Mother's closeness, so I crawled up on the bed and lay close beside her. She lifted the quilts and covered me.

David was much worse by the time Papa and Grandma Rena arrived at dusk. The fire had died down and was almost out. I had used all the stovewood. Papa built up the fire again. Then he carried in stovewood and Grandma Rena built a fire in the wood cookstove.

Grandma had brought a change of clothes in a brown paper bag and her box of snuff that she always used. The dresses she wore were usually orchid or brown and they all had long sleeves. She was the image of neatness. Her auburn hair was pulled back in a soft bun at the back of her head. Grandma was a quiet, gentle lady, often smiling, but I never heard her laugh out loud; and her dark brown eyes held just a hint of some secret sadness that never showed itself.

Baby brother David and me. I'm showing off my Aunt Estelle's watch. I always had wanted to wear it, and finally she gave it to me.

She loved us, but she didn't appreciate our foolishness like Mother and Papa did. We minded her. We knew, too, that she wouldn't hesitate to jerk us up with a sharp slap on our backsides. The household straightened up when she came because we loved and respected her too much to cause her displeasure, or us discomfort. Sometimes when she came to see us, she brought her youngest son, Alden, and we always liked that a lot. But this time it was different.

Dr. Thomas finally came and we watched him examine David. He uncovered just a portion of his tiny body at a time, then covered it up again, to keep the chill of the cold house from touching David's body. When he finished, he looked at Mother and Papa. "He's a very sick child," the doctor said. "David has pneumonia." He left some gray and pink pills and said he would check back the next day.

Papa depended on Grandma Rena in times of trouble and sickness. There was a very special unspoken bond between them. She was there when there was a need, and they worked together as if one knew what the other was thinking.

Grandma Rena and Papa started doctoring. They melted a pill in warm water and gave it to David, just as Dr. Thomas told them to. But when the doctor came back the next day, he told us that David was worse, as we all well knew. He told Papa that he was afraid David wouldn't get better. He was worried, and he said he would be back the next day.

This is how Grandma Rena told this story:

When Lee came back in, he sat for a long time in front of the fire and poked at the logs. Then he got up and walked into the kitchen. He and I sat at the table as he told me what Dr. Thomas had said. I told him to set the skillet on the stove as I got a string of onions and cut them up. We fried onions in lard and made poultices, one for David's back and one for his chest. While Lee fried onions, I rocked David. Then Lee would rock David and I would fry onions. We did this all day and into the next evening. We forced water and tea into his tiny mouth and rubbed his feet with Vicks salve. Avie Lee lay in bed, too sick to rise up, and watched. Denver and Willadeene sat on the foot of her bed. When they finally lay down in the bed beside her, she continued to ask God to spare her son. She was still praying when she went to sleep. Lee and I worked without sleep or rest.

Lee rocked his first-born son as he stared into the fire and listened to the gentle breathing of his other children. Avie Lee would often ask as the night wore on, "Lee, is he going to be all right?" Or, "Is he any better?"

David in his little bib overalls, looking very unhappy.

Grandma Rena's presence brought a feeling of security and a quiet strength. She was always with Mother when all her children were born. She had been there when David was born. The snow was three feet deep that night. Mother was having a real hard time and Papa was scared. He rode his workhorse, Old Bob, to the river to meet Dr. Thomas. The doctor rode the horse back and Lee walked the three miles beside him carrying the doctor's satchel. He walked fast, hurrying to get back to Mother and the children. When they came into the yard, Mother was standing on the porch watching the snow and, of course, watching for Papa to return with the doctor. Grandma Rena couldn't talk Mother back inside the house. But Papa made her get inside. He talked real hateful to her but he didn't mean it; it was just that he was worried about her.

Papa also remembered how I woke up hungry that night and how he'd fried an egg and crumbled corn bread in it. He fed it to me in little bites and gave me milk out of a glass. After I ate, he rocked me back to sleep. He tucked me into my crib bed, which he had moved into the kitchen close to the stove to get me away from the activity in the front room. Then he hurried back to Mother's side after he put more wood on the fires and cleaned the lamp globe that had smoked until the light wasn't bright. They needed light.

Papa had a lot of time to think while he and Grandma cared for his sick family. He was thinking about how he needed to run his trap lines. Maybe his friend Hubert Whaley would drop by and do it for him. He did things like that a lot. He helped with the chores and spoiled me. Hubert was a bachelor, and he teased Papa about being an old married man with all that responsibility and work to do as he helped him burn a tobacco bed. Papa always had a jug behind a stump or leaned up against a tree to take an occasional drink from while they rested. The last batch of whiskey was just awful, and he only drank it because he hadn't had a drink in a good while. He could sure use one now. But Grandma Rena and Mother wouldn't have liked that at all. And he had too much respect for them. This was not the time. They didn't believe in drinking, so he would wait.

Grandma Rena in her flower garden. She loved us so much.

All through the night, the sound of David's labored breathing and fretful cries filled the room. Papa remembers waking up and seeing Grandma Rena on her knees in the kitchen, praying while he had been rocking David in the front room.

Morning came, and while Grandma Rena cooked breakfast, Lee still held David. All of a sudden, David became quiet and limp. Papa called out in a loud voice, "Rena!" Grandma Rena rushed to his side and grabbed David up. Then she smiled at Lee and said, "Praise God, Lee, his fever's broke. He's going to be all right."

When Dr. Thomas came that afternoon, he said he expected to be told that David was dead, for there was no doubt in his mind when he left the day before that it was just a matter of hours before David's lungs would be full of fluid.

So you can see why we grew up believing that if we had God and Grandma Rena, everything would be taken care of.

Dr. Robert F. Thomas. We had God, Grandma Rena, and an occasional visit from Dr. Thomas. That got us through.

The creek was a never-ending source of fun to us. In the winter, a thick layer of ice froze over it where the water was slow moving. We would slide on it for hours. We had ice blisters and skinned places because we didn't always slide across it on our feet.

After a while we would get more and more daring, going closer to the thin ice, until at least two or three of us fell through. The others would drag us out of the icy water and we would try to run to the house. But by the time we got there, our britches would be frozen solid, and we would be stiff-legged, unable to bend our knees or lift our feet.

Once we were inside the house, off would come our frozen clothes and Mother and Papa would wrap us in quilts. Papa would take our soggy shoes and socks off and set them on the hearth to dry. Our feet would look so funny, all red except for the ground-in dirt on our heels. Our hands were always rough and chapped, with dry, black knuckles that wouldn't come clean or smooth until summer.

Mother would get a dishpan of cool water and put our cold, red feet in it. Then she would gradually add hot water from the cast-iron teakettle, saying, "Raise your feet up," as she poured in the water. While she was busy saving our feet from frostbite and our bodies from pneumonia, we were drinking hot ginger tea laced with sugar and whiskey, which she made for us when we got chilled. We loved it. We thought it was a treat. We didn't know at the time it was for sweating out a cold. She would make us sit all bundled up in our quilts close to the fire. Papa would dry our feet and we would put our heels on the hearth with the soles of our feet toward the fire. When we were warm and drowsy, Papa would carry the smaller children to bed and tuck them in with hot-water bottles. Sometimes, he would heat flatirons, wrap them in old shirts, and put them in bed to keep us warm. Jars of hot water were also wrapped and used.

Some winter days were just plain wet and messy. We tracked in mud all day long through the kitchen door. Twenty-two feet can track in a lot of mud. The boys would run through the house and slide in it until Mother opened the door and threw them out on the back porch, daring them to act like they wanted back in.

The kitchen floor was a hazard for anyone who wasn't careful when he or she walked across the strip of thin, slippery mud. It looked almost as bad as the mud hole at the side of the back yard where we threw out the dishwater and where the chickens and pigs hung out looking for food scraps. This mud hole was at the edge of the garden. We not only threw dishwater there, but also all kinds of peelings, corn cobs, pumpkin seeds, and melon rinds.

The chickens could usually be found out there scratching and pecking around. The pigs and ducks were the messy ones, and Mother ended up yelling at us that we were worse than the whole lot of them, as she scrubbed and scrubbed with a broom and tubs of water.

One evening as I watched our nieces play, I couldn't help thinking about when Dolly entered our lives. It snowed the night my sister Dolly was born. I remember Papa taking my brother David and me from our warm beds, putting our coats on us, picking Denver up and putting a quilt around him, and walking with us across the yard to our landlady's house. We didn't want to spend the night there, but since Papa said so, and we were half-asleep, we didn't put up much of a fuss. The three of us slept together in a large feather bed. At dawn, we helped each other dress and hurried back through the snow to our own house.

Papa had not slept, but just to tease us, he let us bang on the door, calling for him to let us in. When we opened the door, I said, "Papa, my baby doll cried all night." He closed the door behind us and said with a smile, "Willadeene, ours did, too."

Papa led me to the bed in the corner of the living room where David and Denver stood by Mother. He pulled the cover back and showed us Dolly. We were sure she was the most beautiful baby in the world. She had blonde hair and blue eyes, and we all had dark hair.

Mother told me I could have her for my very own baby. I took it as serious business, her being my own, and was upset when Denver wanted to know if we had to keep her. Denver had been the baby in the family until then.

It was my responsibility to take care of Dolly. She was a mischievous, curious child, chasing after the gray-and-white kittens that always seemed to be around our house, picking wild flowers, trying to catch butterflies, following me wherever I went.

Like most children, Dolly couldn't keep a secret. We were never supposed to cook when our parents were away from home, because they were afraid we'd get burned. When all the children had crossed their hearts and hoped to die that they wouldn't tell on me, I'd make cookies, cakes, candy, and whatever they wanted. Then Dolly would run to meet Mother and Papa and tell them we didn't do whatever we had actually done.

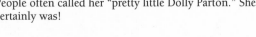

Sometimes older children would take their younger brothers and sisters to school with them. The teachers weren't too happy about this arrangement, but the mothers were because it meant one less child to take care of that day. I loved taking Dolly to school with me before she was old enough to attend her own classes. I would dress her and fix her hair and off we'd go. She would sit in a little chair by me or in the seat with me.

Dolly didn't like school any better than the rest of us, when she finally did start. School was too confining and it didn't offer as much excitement as we could find on our own. Walking to school wasn't any fun either, especially on cold mornings when the frost covered everything in sight. We just never seemed to be able to keep warm in the clothes we had.

It's odd now to see how life seems to repeat itself. We have nieces who are a lot like my sister and me in looks and personality. Dannielle looks and acts a lot like Dolly. I have always been proud to think Donna resembled me. The neices are like extensions of us—through them we can see our young selves once again.

People often called her "pretty little Dolly Parton." She certainly was!

alking to school wasn't any fun on cold mornings when a heavy frost covered the land. We'd dare each other to stick our tongues to the frost-covered mailboxes. Once one of us did, our tongue was stuck there until we pulled it loose, painfully, or waited until the warmth of our tongue and breath melted the ice that held it. We'd usually go ahead and pull it loose because the others were going to run off and leave us there, stuck to the mailboxes! Dolly got her tongue stuck hard once.

Dolly, is there a secret behind that smile?

When we got to school in the morning, we'd go to the cloakroom to hang up our coats and to set our lunches on the overhead shelves that were partitioned off into little boxes about twelve inches square. Our coats hung on nails beneath the shelf. There were benches for us to sit on while we pulled off our overshoes, if we had any; then we put them under the bench until we were ready to go home. The cloakroom had a smell all its own, a sour-sweet smell of food latched up, of wet, not-too-clean coats, and the ever-present odor of fried bacon and woodsmoke that always clung to our clothes in winter.

We often traded our lunches that Mother fixed (biscuits with ham, bacon, or sausage) for a piece of store-bought "light bread" with just mayonnaise on it. One of our favorite things was saltine crackers with chocolate fudge between them. We loved these and would never trade them. We usually ate them on the way to school because we were afraid someone might steal our lunches!

When some of the children got the measles, they also got all the attention. Shades were put over the windows to keep out the strong light, everyonè had to be quiet, and the door had to be kept shut so there wouldn't be a draft.

The older children helped for a while, carrying water, food, and blackberry juice to the sick ones in their bed in front of the fireplace in the front room. Then it began to seem unfair for us to have to do all the work. Some of us wished we could catch the measles again so we would get some attention and some rest. We even went so far as to complain we were dizzy.

When Mother wasn't looking, we leaned our faces close to the fire and then lay back and called Mother to feel our foreheads to see if we had a fever. Mother was smart. She felt our faces and put us to bed as if we were at death's door. She was so attentive to us. She told us how important we were to her and how glad she was that she had children who wouldn't lie to her, that some children pretended to be sick so they wouldn't have to work. But she was so thankful that she didn't have children like that. And she told us that she'd heard of people who pretended to be sick and then they really did get sick and die. But she said that she didn't have to worry about us because if we said we were sick, then we really were.

By that time, it didn't seem like such a good idea to be sick, and we got scared. We knew we couldn't just recover in a minute, so we waited for a while and said, "Mother, I believe I'm better now. You know, I'll bet I sat too close to the fire and just got too hot. Here, let me help you. You go sit down and rest. I'll do that." Mother's psychology never worked on Denver though. So we had to wait on him, too, resenting that we couldn't tell on him.

$\mathcal{U}$ntil we were grown, we never had a turkey for Thanksgiving. We always had chicken or fresh pork. On Thanksgiving Day Papa sometimes killed hogs. We might have chicken, or I should say chickens, because it took more than one to feed all of us! And we might have rabbit if Papa or the boys went hunting. We almost always had slaw, turnip greens and turnips, and chocolate and pumpkin pies. The only turkeys we ever had were the ones that were drawn on orange and brown construction paper. Mother would put them up on the wall when we brought them home from school.

Later, just before the Christmas holidays, all the schools in our area received boxes of used toys and clothes sent by the Mission Board. Every child in school was given a toy and every child was allowed to choose some clothing. Just before we went home for the break, we would each be given two pieces of stick candy, a few nuts, an apple, and sometimes an orange in a brown paper bag.

Birthdays were never a special deal at our house because someone was always having one. The younger children had cake and store-bought ice cream on their birthdays. But sometimes there was only cake, which Mother made, because we didn't always live close to a store.

Once Dolly had a really special little sweetheart who was at our house on his birthday. She liked him so much that she decided to make him a birthday cake. She disappeared into the kitchen for a couple of hours and then reappeared with a bright green birthday cake. The icing was green, the cake was green, and her sweetheart turned green! I don't guess he had ever seen a cake like that before—or since! But we were used to Dolly's ways. After her sweetheart went home, we found his piece of cake hidden under the couch. To this day, Denver still teases Dolly about her running off her beau with a sickening green cake.

ne of the most special things about winter was Christmas. Christmas has a very special meaning for us. It was a time of magic and miracles. Now when I look at a Christmas tree with its flashing lights and bright tinsel, I am taken back to a little mountain cabin and a tree quite different from the ones we usually see today.

Putting up our Christmas tree was one of the most exciting events of the winter, and it involved a week of working in the evenings. First we would go out into the woods and hunt until we found the tree that was just right and pleased everyone. It had to be a cedar tree. Even today, that's the only kind of tree Mother will put up. Everyone who was old enough to walk in the snow would go with Papa, following him and trying to walk in his tracks. He carried the double-bitted axe on his shoulders. We would point out the tree we wanted, and Papa would walk around and around the tree not saying a word, keeping us in a state of uncertainty and excitement. Then he would step back and say, "It looks pretty good to me." With his approval, we would then be excited, too. He would chop the tree off at the ground and drag it all the way home through the snow, making a path for us. We would stick the tree in a bucket of dirt and put it in a corner of the front room.

What fun we had decorating the tree! We even

Dolly holding a new relative.

helped make the decorations. And we loved making candy, gingerbread men, strings of popcorn, and strings of colored buttons. Mother made little bells out of the gold and silver paper from gum and tobacco wrappers she had saved throughout the year. And we would dip pine cones in flour water. After they dried and were placed on the tree, they looked like they were covered in snow.

When the tree was decorated and we were all satisfied that it was the best ever, Mother would tell us the Christmas story of the birth of Christ. We would dress up in quilts and curtains and act out each part. It was a serious play, and we did our very best because Papa was our audience. Then Papa would have Mother sing for us. In her haunting, pure, mountain voice, she would sing "Silent Night," "O Little Town of Bethlehem," "O Beautiful Star of Bethlehem," and "Away in a Manger." Papa said she was better than Mother Maybelle or Kitty or any of the Opry stars. He felt that he had his own Opry right at home, complete with back-up singers.

One Christmas Eve, we went to the barn to watch the animals kneel at midnight. We walked single file across the snow, the boys leading the way. We hollowed out a big hole deep in the hay and sat there wrapped in our quilts with just our noses and eyes showing. We were determined that we wouldn't fall asleep before midnight. As we waited, one or two got fidgety and went back to the house. The rest of us waited patiently for the magic hour. We waited and waited and waited. The next thing we knew, Papa was there, shaking us awake and saying, "Come on, kids," and we knew then that we had missed seeing the animals kneel in reverence to the birth of Christ. We were a disappointed, scraggly group as Papa led us back to the house. Next Christmas, we promised each other, we would be sure to stay awake!

Each of the older children would hang a stocking on the mantel, and years later, when the younger ones were ready for Santa Claus, they would leave one of their red or green cowboy boots on the hearth instead of hanging a stocking.

When we would wake up on cold winter mornings, some of us would always ask, "Can we get up?" before we got out of the bed, or "Papa, is the fire hot yet?" Christmas morning came and there was a chorus of expectant voices: "Papa, is the fire hot yet?" We'd be raising ourselves up, trying to see our stockings, trying to see if there was anything in them. Finally, he'd say, "Yeah." Then we'd all scramble out of bed and run to the front room.

Trembling with excitement, we'd look in our stockings first, and we'd find a stick of candy, an orange, an apple, English walnuts, and chocolate drops. We could see some presents under the tree, but we had to wait until after breakfast before we could open them. Sometimes Mother made hot cocoa and chocolate rolls and cinnamon rolls for Christmas breakfast. Giant icicles would be hanging on the edge of the roof and the sun made them sparkle and glisten. We'd sit and sip our cocoa and pretend

When Papa cut the cellophane wrapper from the candy box, the wonderful smell of chocolate filled the air.

we were kings and queens living in a diamond palace. Then we'd hear the snow on the roof begin to slide off. As it moved over the edge of the tin roof, off came the icicles together with the snow, and it all plopped to the ground.

We always had at least one store-bought present from Papa and Mother. Mother would buy Papa a pack of bandanna handkerchiefs and a box of chocolate-covered cherries. Papa wouldn't open his box of candy until days later, after the children had forgotten about it. Then some night after supper, he would get it out and carefully cut the cellophane wrapper with his pocketknife. We'd sit there, watching each slow movement as he took his time taking the cellophane off and slowly opening the box. Each one of us was given a chocolate-covered cherry, still in its little paper cup. I don't think he ever ate a piece of it himself. Instead, he saved it for us to enjoy.

*D*olly loves her family and shows it in so many ways, with her words and letters, and by the generous things she does. She wants all of us to be happy and does what she can to help. One instance of her generosity and love came to pass years after the original promise was made.

Before Dolly went to Nashville, Papa had to sell the house he and Mother had built because they needed money. Mother hadn't wanted to sell and was so unhappy with the old farmhouse we moved to. One day she was crying and Dolly said, "Don't worry about it, Mama. As soon as I make enough money, I'll buy it back for you."

Years later, not only did she buy the house back for Mother, but she also completely remodeled the house. She added two rooms, a Ben Franklin stove-fireplace, paneling, new floors, and bricking for the entire outside of the house. But Dolly didn't stop there. That same year, for Mother and Papa's Christmas present, Dolly completely refurnished the house.

Dolly came home, and we did most of the shopping in Knoxville. It took a few days because Dolly bought everything—curtains, pictures, dishes, and all the furniture. We all helped her. It wasn't an easy job keeping Mother and Papa away all day and way into the night. Aunt Estelle, Mother's sister, and her husband, Uncle Dot Watson, persuaded them to go home with them so they wouldn't know what was going on until we got the furniture delivered and the house put together.

Our brothers, David, Denver, Bobby, Floyd, and Randy, emptied the house of all the old things while Carl, Arthur, Larry, and Carroll went to bring home all the new furniture. Our brothers' wives, Pat, Doris, and Carolyn, worked just as hard as we did. They pressed drapes and helped hang them, washed windows, put things in the new chest of drawers and dressers, and hung pictures.

Around noon, Carl, Arthur, Carroll, and Larry brought the furniture, and we ate the lunch Pat and Doris had cooked for us. The house began to take shape around five o'clock, so some of us started decorating the Christmas tree. While the men put the Christmas lights on the outside of the house, we were working inside. We hadn't forgotten anything on our shopping spree. When everything was finished, Dolly wanted to fix up, so she put on a red

Left to right: Randy, Mother, Floyd, Papa, and Rachel. Deb, and Tever.

velvet jumpsuit. We called her Santa and told her that the elves were too tired to get fixed up.

A neighbor came in and played Santa. Dot and Estelle came home with Mother and Papa to see everything we had done. All the work was well worth it when we saw the looks of surprise and joy on their faces. They had known we were up to something, but they never suspected this! Mother still had to have a cedar Christmas tree, which she and her grandchildren put up in another part of the house to decorate their way.

We had a beautiful Christmas, because we were all together and enjoyed each other. We teased and reminisced. We sang Christmas carols and every other kind of song. We even had a good time telling all the mean and silly things we did when we were growing up. As Dolly worked, she sang "Tall Man" and "Puppy Love" until we were begging her to stop, like we had done when she was on the Cas Walker show. She was just doing it to tease us now.

Denver used to tell her, "Ah, you think you can sing as good as Brenda Lee." It would hurt her feelings but she was just his silly sister. (I think Denver had a crush on Brenda Lee anyway.) He has always aggravated Dolly, but he loves her and named his first child Dolly Christina after her.

Papa, Dolly, and Mother.

*J*ust after Dolly left home, she moved into a trailer. One Christmas, Cassie and Stella went to visit her. They were excited about decorating the trailer. Dolly has always gone to extremes because she wants everything decorated to fit the occasion. If it's Christmas, then *everything* has to look like Christmas.

They went shopping and came back loaded down with decorations. They put up the tree and then strung tinsel and ornaments in every room, including the kitchen and bathroom. They put red bulbs in all the light sockets and lamps. To complete the decorating, they hung a wreath with a big red bow outside on the door and put a red bulb in the outside light fixture.

With all this done, it was time to wrap packages. They sat in the middle of the floor surrounded by Christmas paper and bows, laughing and talking as they wrapped presents. Someone knocked on the door and when Dolly asked, "Who's there?" the person wouldn't answer. The girls peeped out the window as a man walked away. This happened again, but it was a different man. They finally decided the men were a couple of drunks who had mistaken their trailer for someone else's, and they thought no more about it.

Then Uncle Bill and Carl came over. Bill held up the red light bulb he had taken from the porch and said, "What the hell do you think you're doing?" Then he and Carl pushed by the girls and went from room to room unscrewing all their pretty light bulbs.

Bill realized that the girls didn't know any better. So he and Carl sat them down and explained that red lights didn't always represent the Christmas spirit, but sometimes something quite different!

Dolly was hurt by their attitude and upset because of the mistake she'd made. But not to be outdone, she said, "But we've already had two visitors!" (Dolly loves to shock people.) The crisis was over and the tension broken. Everybody set about teasing and speculating on ways to use a dozen red light bulbs.

*W*hen Dolly and Carl were first married, they came to Sevierville a lot. They usually stayed at my house because I had moved into an old farmhouse and had plenty of room. Sometimes, when Dolly was on the road, Carl would come to Sevierville to see his in-laws by himself. He and Arthur would go to the races, or cattle auctions, or he would go to the construction job with Arthur. In the winter, they would cut wood for the fireplace and maybe work on the farm equipment.

Dolly and Carl during the first year they were married.

Lots of times, Cassie and her husband, Larry Seaver, and Stella and her husband, Carroll Rauhuff, would come with Carl and Dolly when they could all take off work at the same time. The girls would get up early and cook breakfast. Dolly would always say, "Deene, you make the biscuits and I'll make the gravy, 'cause I make better gravy than you do." But she doesn't.

As soon as we could get the men fed, we'd shoo them out of the house to do whatever they wanted to do, just as long as they got out from under our feet so that we could do whatever we wanted to. Finally it got so that we didn't have to worry. They were always going somewhere. But we liked it, because they were doing what they wanted to do and so were we.

Our men would always go over to Mother and Papa's at least once a day, to talk to Papa and to tease and aggravate Mother. They'd go in saying, "Mother-in-law, have you got some coffee?" She'd fix coffee and almost always ask, "Where's the girls?" Then they'd start. "We're looking for them. They didn't come home last night and we thought they'd stayed over here!" And sometimes they could really get her going until she realized they were teasing. They'd say, "See you, Mother-in-law," and leave. Mother enjoyed every minute of their teasing, although she wouldn't ever admit it to them. Even the fact that they called her "Mother-in-law" instead of Mrs. Parton tickled her.

$\mathcal{M}$other has ESP. If you met her, you wouldn't think she was ever still or stopped talking long enough to receive or send any messages. She doesn't work at it at all, and mostly it involves just her family.

She can often tell us things that are going to happen to us. She can tell if something is going to be good or bad for us. She can often tell us if we should be careful about certain people or ventures. We trust her with these feelings. She never discourages us in any way, but always encourages us. She attributes this foresight to her deep faith in God and believes it's His way of giving her help and solace in a time of need.

Mother and Papa also have a sense of humor and they thought the things we did as children were funny. We'd hear them laughing and talking about something we had done when they thought we weren't around. I guess with a family our size and with such a mixture of personalities, we had to have a sense of humor.

We have had as much fun about Mother and Papa as they have had about us. The first time they were ever on an airplane, Mother sat and prayed silently and Papa took a big drink. When Mother finished praying, she started in on Papa, telling him that he ought to be praying instead of drinking whiskey and that the plane could crash. Papa said, "Damn it to hell, Avie Lee, I'm scared enough already!"

One Christmas we had gathered at their house to

Bobby, Dolly, Heidi, and Rebecca during a Christmas TV special.

spend the holidays with them. We got there just fine, but Mother was not there! She had flown to Oklahoma the evening before for a vacation with Aunt Dorothy Jo. We had never had a Christmas without Mother. So we sat around with Papa, trying to have Christmas without her. The more we worked at it, the funnier it got.

Papa sat in his big brown recliner and didn't say much as we all began arriving with our families. No Mother meant no Christmas dinner. All of us girls had to cook because we couldn't bear to think that our Papa didn't have anyone to fix dinner for him—or us.

Well, Mother had really done it this time! We all petted Papa to pretend that everything was normal. At least Mother had done one thing right. Before she left, she had gotten him his usual Christmas present—a box of chocolate-covered cherries and a bandanna.

As we cooked dinner, Dolly decided she would be Mother. Of all of us, she can act the most like Mother and can even talk like her. She almost ruined our food by going around adding this and adding that. By the time the day was

Left to right: Darlene Williams, Stella, Papa, and Mother. Mother and Papa had flown to Washington to see Stella. This was their first time to fly.

Above: four generations. *Left to right:* Dena, Jordan, me, and Mother.

Right: Mother taking a spin on Mitchell's bike.

over we still missed Mother, but we enjoyed Christmas anyway.

Then Stella remembered the "dumb supper" and decided we'd have one. I'd forgotten about it, and the younger ones had never heard of it. So Stella explained to them as she set the table and put the food on it. Bread and water—nothing else. Since I was divorced at the time, the purpose of the dumb supper was to find a husband for me. I got tickled because I am a matter of concern to them all since I am single. They've introduced me to doctors, lawyers, judges, singers, writers, senators, congressmen, professors, army generals, actors, and fortune hunters. I've been a source of worry and made a lot of fun for them. And my son, Mitchell, tells them he feels just like a father because he has to worry about me. He tells my boyfriends when they call that I can't talk to them because I'm grounded for staying out past my curfew. Mitchell goes on my dates with me sometimes because, he says, he wants to see what middle-aged puppy love looks like. People used to call Denver and ask him for my phone number. He'd say, "What in the hell do you think this is, a damn lonely hearts club?"

Well, Stella had decided to change all that. The dumb supper was supposed to determine who my husband will be. This is something that people used to play years ago to entertain each other. This is how it's done: The table is set and bread and water are the meal. Everyone comes to the table and sits down to eat. No one can say anything or laugh; it's serious business. They proceed with the supper and the first man who comes to the door is supposed to be the husband. We modified our dumb supper a bit and sat at our table with some very good wine and the best breads we'd ever tasted. No one came. So I go on alone, or as alone as I can be with all those brothers and sisters and a son.

Beautiful Stella gets all the phone calls, not me.

When I look around, a lot of things I have are gifts from my family. Randy and his family have always been generous to me, as well as others. I can always count on beautiful sweaters and shirts and anything they think I'd like or need. Stella, Rachel, Hannah, and Mother do the same thing. They all know I don't like to buy for myself. Dolly has given me a house, a couple of cars, and clothes (not just an outfit or two, but an entire wardrobe).

A few years ago for my Christmas present she went shopping at Tiffany's. She bought me a beautiful silver and pink crystal angel necklace. I had no idea what she was doing, but I was painting a watercolor of angels and crystals. I did a couple of them. Hannah has one in her room. I had it framed in red, blue, and yellow. Dolly's gift to me was wrapped in the same colors. Even the card I got from her was the same colors. Sometimes it seems uncanny that we can be on so many of the same wavelengths.

Even though we were all afraid this past winter when Denver was so sick, we had to laugh at his spunk. He had major abdominal surgery, twice within a ten-day period. When he had been in the hospital for six weeks, Cassie and Rachel made one of their visits to him. He immediately asked for a cup of hot coffee. Cassie reminded him he was not allowed to have coffee yet. "Well," Denver retorted, "the least you could do is bring me a cup and wave it back and forth under my nose so I could smell it!"

Being uneasy and afraid for him, and trying to lighten the situation, Cassie told him that maybe she should get even with him for all the things he did to her as a child. Through his pain and clinched teeth he stayed true to his personality and said, "I don't know if you want to do that. I might live!"

I'm glad to say Denver is fully recovered and mean as ever.

*G*reat-grandson Jordan, Dena's baby, was so excited about the snow this past year that he had to be brought to Mother and Papa's house to snowfight. He was really into this for the first time. He kept telling his Mamaw to hit him in the face with a snowball, so she was throwing snow in his face.

He said, "Mamaw, lay down in the snow and make me a Mamaw Angel." He and Dena had been making mommy and baby snow angels. When Mother figured out what he meant, she said, "Jordan, you're talking to the wrong Mamaw. I don't even make angel cookies anymore, much less snow angels. You better call Mama Deene or Aunt Granny (Dolly). Why, I wouldn't be able to get up out of the yard till spring."

Above (left to right): Judy Ogle, Dolly, and Jada. Everyone can depend on Dolly to help out when there is a new baby.

My son, Mitchell, and me.

At our Christmas party in 1995, we started talking about kids' accidents and especially how no one seemed to make it to adulthood without burning themselves at least once. This conversation made Mitchell recall a teacher he really disliked. Mitchell had gotten burned and was crying to come home, and she told him to call me. He told her he didn't know our number. She said, "You don't know your own phone number?" (This was his first year of school.) He piped up, "No, I never call myself!"

Another time, when Mitchell was in the fifth grade, the teacher asked him how he expected to have a job and keep up a family if he couldn't spell any better than he did. He looked real serious at her and said, "I will have a secretary to do that, and I'm going to live with my mother or build me a house right across her driveway!"

Stella's son, Tim, used to stay with Mother and me a lot when he was

Kathy, my daughter-in-law, and my son, Mitchell.

Uncle Wayne Ball and Hannah.

Precious Heidi, always smiling like
Aunt Granny (Dolly).

Christmas is family time for us. *Left to right:* Heidi
and Tever in front, with Deb and Randy in back.

small. Stella worked and she went to cosmetology school. One time Tim got a
burn on the back of his hand. Well, Mother did all she could for his pain,
including praying for it. Finally she brought him to my house. I headed to the
drugstore to get something to stop the pain and to Remacs drive-in for a
burger and fries. Surely that would help.

He was really in pain, so I said as we drove along, "Tim, honey, let's pray
again," hoping to give him some comfort. He said, "If God were going to help
me, he would have done something when Mamaw prayed." So much for my
good intentions. I realized that if God wouldn't do it for Mamaw, I didn't need
to waste my time.

Jada thinks this may be a joke—Mama Deene and Santa making a list and checking it twice.

Lately, I have helped the children grow a magic garden. I tell them to throw the seed into the yard and a Magic Christmas Garden will grow. During Christmas 1994, the garden had a Santa in green-and-white papier-mâché and a sleigh of the most unusual and beautiful material you've ever seen. Floyd made it.

The children raided the garden over and over again. There was a tree with lollipops as big as Frisbees, wisteria vines hanging full of candy canes, lights, and toys. The ground was covered with lights shining through glitter and snow, with gingerbread boys and girls with the children's names on them. If your name is in the garden and the bells are ringing and music is playing, you can take whatever you like from the garden.

The children can't be brought to my house unless it's dark, because that is when the garden is magic. In one part of the garden are an elf and a Santa and some real reindeer. Off to the other side of the yard is a large decorated pine tree. It has all kinds of food for the animals and birds in baskets of hand-woven honeysuckle vines and a star of twigs and straw. The prettiest tree we've ever had, it represents the tree Diana Rhea's song is about, called "Paw Prints in the Snow." We have had different farm animals and house pets around it at different times.

This past year we sowed the garden right after Thanksgiving dinner. Each child planted a handful of "magic seeds" and had to wait until Christmas to see what they grew. Rebecca, one of the grandchildren, sowed and raked along with the others. She came in from the cold, dusting off her hands. When asked if she had planted, she propped her hands on her hips and said, "Yes. But I doubt that any magic will grow." She was the most thrilled and excited of all the children when she returned at Christmas. She had forgotten about it completely. We will do this garden again and again.

Dolly and Jada both getting a hug. Heidi waiting to give Aunt Granny (Dolly) a hug and a gift.

Wonder whose idea it was to get all dressed up. *Left to right:* Freida, Cassie, and Rachel in front, and Stella, Dolly, and me in the back.

Spring

The shining spring sun on the laurel
trees looks radiant, like the look
of one in love.
The few remaining leaves of the oak
trees endured the cruel winter
wind and cold.
They're like an old lady who has
endured many seasons, but
they giggle like schoolgirls,
out loud and unashamed,
in the spring breeze as if
only waiting to see life
begin all over again.
The tender young buds shyly peek
out from under their warm blanket.
Sometimes the frost pinches their
tiny pink noses and they stay
covered a few more days.

$\mathcal{W}$e were pretty sure that it was almost spring when our cupboards and cellar started getting bare. We had enjoyed winter but usually we had just about all of it that we could stand. We'd been cooped up for months and desperately wanted the freedom that spring brought us.

The honeybees would start coming out and hanging on the sides of the hives in the warm, thin sunshine. They'd feed on the sugar water that Mother and Papa set around the hives for them to find. Papa always kept bees and sold the honey. One time I remember he was finding dead bees near the creek, and he worried that they were getting poison from somewhere. We knew the long winter was really over when Papa came from the woods and announced, "The sarvis is blooming!"

Lettuce, radishes, mustard, turnip greens, and volunteer onions were coming up. All the wonderful things began to grow again—watercress and dry-land cress, poke salat, speckled dock, and lamb's-quarters. Papa would let us go with him when he picked the wild greens to take home to cook with fatback. He knew all the edible plants, but we never did pay much attention to what he picked. We just wanted to go with him.

Then the redbuds were blooming and the blue-and-white violets. The little flowers that looked like miniature white violets, that we called Johnny-jump-ups, were everywhere.

We prowled the creekbanks looking for duck eggs. Our feet were always wet in our now worn-out shoes. Our shirts had patches, and extensions had been sewn on the legs of our britches to compensate for growth during the long winter. The boys needed a haircut, and Papa got to that as soon as he had time.

Papa always planted by the old signs. It was time to plant corn when we heard the first whippoorwill. If the groundhog saw his shadow February 14 (old Groundhog Day), there would be six more weeks of bad weather.

Potatoes were planted in February or March by the dark of the moon—during the days of the month of the old moon. February was the month when we piled brush in long, narrow piles higher than our heads for tobacco beds. Papa would set this afire and we'd all tend it and watch that it didn't set the woods on fire. When it burned down, we'd rake the dirt and ashes smooth for

Dolly and Cas Walker, her first boss. It's hard to tell who is enjoying this show the most.

Papa to sow the tiny tobacco seeds. He always left one end of the bed to sow tomatoes, cabbage, lettuce, and peppers. Then we'd outline the long bed with logs and nail canvas over it to protect the tiny seedlings when they came up. In April or May the tobacco plants would be transplanted to the tobacco patch and the vegetable plants would be planted in our newly plowed garden.

We all helped with the transplanting, which usually took about a week to finish. In the afternoons it was hot, and as soon as Papa said our day's work was over we would run to the creek and cool off, swimming in the refreshing mountain water.

One evening in the mid 1940s, the rain started shortly after supper. All through the night it beat with a steady, incessant roar against the tin roof. Cooking pots, buckets, dishpans, and tubs were set in the different rooms where we knew the "hard rain" leaks were. But this time there were new leaks. There would be the sound of "splat, splat" and Mother would get out of bed, light the oil lamp, and set another bucket under the new leak.

About midnight a new, more frightening sound began. At first it was hardly noticeable, but it grew in intensity until it drowned out all other sounds. The faraway low roar came closer and then it filled the house. It was the sound of streams overflowing their banks, churning with a fury that can only be watched helplessly. The friendly, lazy little branches and creeks, some only a few feet wide, became monstrous torrents of death and destruction. With the sound came horrible, helpless fear.

These were the spring floods that came every year in the mountains and still do. Some are more destructive than others, but there is no way of knowing the loss until the waters subside. Morning came and even the downpour of the rain was silenced by the flood. Everywhere, the muddy water swirled and tumbled. Cows and horses huddled on small islands that, before the rain, had been hilltops. Chickens were stranded in the trees where they had roosted for the night. A few of the more timid ones had spent the night under the house and now stood on the edge of the porch, wet and bewildered.

David, Denver, and I got up earlier than usual. We dumped the water from the pans and buckets and replaced them under the leaks. Mother cooked breakfast and we ate in silence. If there was a conversation, it was only between Mother and Papa in subdued, hushed voices. There were the almost-whispered words of "I wonder if the neighbors are all right?" The usually boisterous younger kids sat wide-eyed and still. It was almost as if they were afraid any noise would cause the flood to descend its wrath upon the little house, which for the moment was secure.

After breakfast was over, Papa sat down in a straightbacked chair by the fireplace and pulled his galoshes on over his boots. I knew he was going out in the flood and I choked back the tears that were burning my eyes. I was so afraid for him to go. Mother handed him his coat and hat and he opened the

This entire family lost their lives in the flood of 1938 in Sevier County.

door, turned and looked at all of us, and then he was gone. He would follow the ridge for miles to see if any of our neighbors were in trouble. If he could get down to the houses, he knew the people inside were safe. A certain route that was his "flood route" extended for miles. Other men in the community walked their routes, so that there could be no doubt that all the families in the community were safe. One family's house was surrounded by water, but Papa saw the people up at their barn. They waved to him that they were all right. He couldn't talk to them because no one could hear above the loud roar of the water. We found out later that they had made it to the barn just as the water began surrounding their house.

While Papa was gone, the little ones huddled around Mother for solace. I kept busy by cleaning up the breakfast dishes and letting the tears finally come now that Papa was not there to see me. We couldn't bear the thought of our Papa being out there. What if something happened to him? But even then I knew the kind of man he was and loved him for it. He had to help his neighbors, and he is that way today.

As the flood swirled outside, Mother began to tell a story. Everything important that happened in our lives, she would relate to a story in the Bible. We listened intently as she again told us the story of Noah, the ark, and the rainbow.

Then we begged Mother to tell us about the flood of 1938, when eight people were washed away in the aftermath of a cloudburst. One entire family of six was swept away when the engorged underground streams exploded out of a mountainside. The bodies of the family were found in different places downstream from their home. When Mother came to the part about the little dead baby found in a rose bush, we all cried, knowing how much we loved our own little baby, Dolly.

Within a week, the streams were back to normal and life went on as before. The reprieve Mother and Papa had enjoyed from all our fights was now at an abrupt end.

~

When spring was at its fullest, fruit trees everywhere were heavy with bloom. Pear and wild plum trees were full of white blossoms. Apple trees promised a good harvest by the pale pink blooms worked so lovingly by the bees.

All the many different kinds of butterflies tried their silky new wings in the warm spring air. Frogs heralded spring in a never-ending chorus from the ponds and ditches. We went to sleep and awoke to the sound of birds. We enjoyed spring to the fullest for we knew that summer, with all the work it demanded, would soon appear.

We loved seeing all the new animal babies—the wobbly calves, the quick, curious piglets, and the fluffy little ducks. Our neighbors owned sheep and we were fascinated by the soft, playful lambs but intimidated by the rams. There were ordinarily two or three fat old hens wanting to set. They'd walk around for days clucking and ruffling their feathers at everything that moved before they finally "took to the nest" and stayed there most of the time. Papa would take a "settin'" of eggs, mark them with a pencil, and put them in each of their nests. Some of the other hens would lay eggs in the setting hens' nests and we had to check every evening and take them away from the marked settings. We tried to get the fresh eggs out when the setting hens came off their nests to eat; otherwise, they would flog our arms and hands. An old setting hen doesn't peck—she wrings hunks out of you!

After twenty-eight days, the chicks began to hatch. If we felt brave, we'd scare the mother hen off the nest and watch the chicks hatch until the old hen got so violently upset we'd have to leave. Her attitude didn't improve, but worsened, after the little brood was hatched and began following her around. We stayed pretty much out of her way and so did the dogs and cats after they suffered a few surprise attacks and confrontations.

Last spring I was hurrying about one day thinking only of the errands I needed to run and that I needed to drive into town. I put Saatchi, my dog, in the car and out of the corner of my eye I spied a butterfly in the impatiens. I was instantly transported to my childhood daydreams and remembered how important all our dreams were to us. We tried to outdream one another, and we never even suspected that our dreams wouldn't come true. We are still dreamers today, and reality is sometimes an inconvenience that has to be moved aside or overcome if it doesn't fit our dreams. Now I think it's called denial.

The harshness of our lives and the lack of material wealth were softened because our minds always whispered, "Someday . . . someday. . . ." We lived in castles long before we'd ever seen one. We wore fairy-tale clothes in rainbow colors before we'd read about Paris.

The fact that we played make-believe wasn't unusual because most children do, but we held on to our dreams because we never learned how to let them go. They are a necessary part of our lives and sometimes are more real to us than reality.

If something we want and expect doesn't happen when we think it should, we grieve and worry and finally accept the philosophy Mother taught us: "It is not the time. Be patient. If you believe strongly enough, it will happen." She would point out things in nature and how different phases of growth had to take place before something was complete—like the tadpoles that had to go through a lot of different changes that took time before they became what God intended. And how the butterfly didn't just appear but had to wait for a while in the darkness of the cocoon until the time was right and everything was

Dolly and a couple of her many butterflies.

ready. Its wings, which were made strong from the waiting, carried it wherever it wanted to go.

We were never ridiculed by our parents, and they were the ones whose opinions were important to us. We grew up in total freedom to express ourselves, and our creative efforts were treated as masterpieces by Mother and Papa. Now we know they thought we were a bunch of clowns who made them laugh and smile. But we always had an appreciative audience, with no harsh criticism to destroy the belief in our talents.

Saatchi, my best pal, was given to me by my late husband, Raymond.

All the sisters with Floyd and Randy on Randy's front porch.

*O*ur grandparents and great-grandparents were a continuing source of stability and love. We all liked to visit Grandma Rena and Grandpa Jake, especially in the spring or on the days that Homer Greene's rolling store went by. We liked to go with Grandma Rena when she bought a few things she needed. The rolling store was a big blue-and-white bus. Shelves full of all kinds of things that people might need lined the walls, and there were chicken cages on the sides. Grandma sold chickens and eggs to the man to pay for what she needed. She had us watch for him even though he stopped at every house. We'd sound the alarm by yelling, "Here comes the peddler. Hurry, hurry, Grandma. Here he comes!"

I especially recall how Grandma Parton loved Poppy and how devoted he was to her. He wouldn't eat until he was sure she had her food just exactly as she wanted it. Even in the later years, when Uncle Leonard and Aunt Doris took care of them, his first thought was to make sure Grandma was first in everything.

Grandma Parton and Dolly always had a special bond. Even after she was grown, Dolly bought beautiful expensive jewelry, cosmetics, and wigs for Grandma. I can see now that they loved the same things. Dolly was so pleased that she could give Grandma Parton special things she enjoyed but had never had

Dolly owns this bus now, along with the books showing where Mr. Greene let people buy food on credit. Mother and Papa's names are there.

before. Dolly would visit her when she had a few days off the road and they were like two little girls. Grandma would dress up and put on her brown wig. Then Dolly would fix it just right. She would help Grandma put on makeup, taking as much care as she did with her own. Those two would spend all day in their makeup and wigs. Dolly loved doing these special things for her because Grandma enjoyed it so much. I sometimes wonder if she didn't enjoy just having Dolly fuss over her and having Dolly completely to herself.

Dolly still sings on stage some of her older songs she sang for Grandma Parton.

Grandma loved to hear Dolly sing her latest songs, and she sat enthralled as Dolly talked about the parties she'd been to and the trips she'd made, describing them in detail to Grandma, who'd never been beyond the mountains.

After Grandma died, Aunt Doris sent all the jewelry that Dolly had given Grandma back to her. Dolly put it away with the pictures and mementos of Grandma that she treasures and will be able to look at again someday when the pain of losing her is not as strong.

Grandma Valentine, our great-grandmother, taught me how to make sachets to put in the chests with our sheets and quilts and in the dresser drawers with our clothes to make them smell good.

We'd pull the outer petals off flowers and dry them on a piece of tin in the sun. When they were dry, we mixed them with orris root and added cloves, cinnamon, or ginger and tied the mixture up in small cloths. Grandma grew lavender just for sachets.

She also raised a lot of herbs to use in her cooking, but I think she really just liked having them because very few women had herb gardens. Most people had garlic and dill and perhaps sage, but Grandma added uncommon ones, like rosemary, thyme, chives, basil, and fennel.

The fences around the hen house had gourds of all descriptions growing against them, climbing to the tops of the rails. The most exciting vine Grandma grew was what we called a "pomegranate." It had beautiful, perfectly round fruit with a smooth skin of burnt orange color and vertical yellow stripes. The fragrance of the pomegranate is like nothing else, sweet but not flowerlike. We loved its heady aroma like cats love catnip. I remember the beauty of the flowers and their strong fragrances in the hot sun and how in the cool of the evenings their scent would become faint and subtle.

Grandma Valentine hadn't been able to go to school except for a short time. She was needed at home to help with the housework and the work in the fields, so she never learned to read. Nevertheless, throughout her life she kept the desire to learn. Wesley, her youngest son, and his wife, Edna, lived with Grandma and took care of her. When Wesley's children started school, they would come home and share their books and knowledge with Grandma; so Jean, Dora, and Grandma learned to read together. This had been one of her greatest desires for more than half a century—to read her Bible and all the books she wanted to.

*T*here are so many things that make life wonderful, especially stories from relatives like my great-aunt Lillie. She is sort of the family historian. Since she was born in the late 1800s, she remembers so many things I love to hear.

She tells how Mother was always stubborn and independent even as a child, and relates stories that Mother has never told us: How Mother ran away from home because Grandpa Jake had forbidden her to see Papa again. Girls didn't do that sort of thing back then. Grandpa decided to let them get married after that.

She also tells how after I was born Mother would wrap me in a blanket and take me on long walks in the woods and the fields where we lived. Aunt Lillie says she always worried about me and Mother because Mother was so young. She would tell Grandma Rena and Grandma Lindy that Mother was going to lose me.

Now, when she talks about it, she tells me that of course Mother wasn't going to lose me, that she never laid me down. When Mother sat down, she would put me on her lap. If she lay down in the grass and clover, she would lay me on her chest. Aunt Lillie knows this because she used to follow Mother, looking out for us. She says that if Mother saw her, she would just wait for Aunt Lillie to catch up and they would walk along together. I Love thinking how sweetly I was cared for, even before I could remember.

~

*N*ow that we are scattered and can't see each other as often as we would like, we find we long to be together. As Stella says in this letter I received last spring, now our "dreams" frequently turn to being with each other and sharing our lives more closely:

May 1995
Dearest Willadeene,

I finally have the time to sit down and write you a note. We have just finished our second successful season at the Hat House Cafe. Whew! It's a lot of work running a business and working the road. I am pleased to have a break.

I am very happy your book is being published. A lot of people ask for a book about us when I am signing autographs. I'm still amazed that people are so curious about our family. If they only knew—we are just like everyone else.

Thanks for sending the corn bread, fried potatoes, and vegetable soup. How did you know I would be too busy to eat? I guess you know me better than I think you do.

I sure enjoyed my birthday party with Cassie, Rachel, and you this year. Even if you did laugh at me for asking to borrow your reading glasses to read the menu. I almost didn't mind turning a year older. I still want to take you out for your birthday.

As you know, Tim has graduated from college and is now on his own. I am so proud of him. He has always been my greatest joy as Mitchell is to you. It really is wonderful to see how blessed we are as a family. I do thank God every day.

Mom and Dad are still doing well as they march on into their mid-seventies. It's great to see Hannah doing so well after her illness. I am glad you were there for Rachel, Richard, and her throughout her treatments. As always, I was off on the road working and wasn't much help. It's a good thing there are so many of us to help out in a crisis! It seems you always wade in the deepest. I guess that's what being the "Mama Deene" is all about.

Remember the time when I stayed with you when I was sick with my kidney problems and you nursed me back to health. Mama didn't need a sick kid around with all she had going on. I even enjoyed your fussing over me. You know, I was never comfortable being fussed over and spoiled by anyone but you. You never made it seem like a bother or a duty. It was almost like a joy for you to look after someone in need. God does put "special angels" in our lives and you are definitely one to me. You are the best "Mama Deene"—the only "Mama Deene."

I've got to stop daydreaming and get this letter in the mail or you won't get it until next year. Sometime let's get together for a few days and catch up. I need a sister fix as only you can give. In case I forgot to tell you or show you often enough, I love you and respect you with all my heart. You are the truest sister anyone could ever have. I love you, "Mama Deene."

Love,
Stella ("Teda")

Left to right: Angie (Bobby's wife), Bobby, Dolly, and Tim (Stella's son).

Aunt Estelle, Dolly, and me.

Some of the most exciting times of our growing up were when Aunt Dorothy Jo and Aunt Estelle would come to visit us. They were Mother's sisters and we all loved them dearly. They told us about all kinds of interesting things, like places they worked, going on trips to other states, movies, new fashions, the war, sweethearts, and going to the carnival, where they had their fortunes told by gypsies.

I recall one visit they made in late March, when the dogwood and redbud were both in bloom. Dorothy Jo and Estelle showed us neat things to do, like writing our sweethearts' names on little pieces of paper and then rolling them up in balls of meal dough. We'd drop them all in a pint jar full of water. When the meal balls dissolved, the paper that came up to the top first was supposed to be the one who loved us most. But we couldn't stop at that, we had to know who loved us next best and next best until all the names had come to the top.

They told us how to pull the wishbone of the chicken. We called them "pulley bones." Whoever got the short piece would marry first. The girl who got the short pulley bone would prop it above the door. The first boy who walked under it was to be the one she'd marry. Whenever Dolly's pulley bone was above the door, she'd watch real close and if some boy she didn't like came, she would jerk it down before he walked under it and put up my pulley bone, or Stella's or Cassie's.

We did these silly games until we were in our teens. We didn't have TV, movies, very many books, video games, arcades, McDonald's, bungee jumps, racetracks, Dollywood, or anything else children have today.

Sometimes some of us got to go home with our aunts for a few days. We were in our glory! As we got older, they would let the girls wear their pretty clothes and use their makeup and perfume. If it hadn't been for them caring so very much for us, we wouldn't have had all the little "extras" that are so important to teenage girls.

They laughed with us, cried with us, and, most important, listened to us as if we were grown up. They encouraged our dreams, as did Mother and Papa, and they shared our secrets that we couldn't trust to anyone else.

Dolly gives Aunt Doris (Papa's sister-in-law) a hug.

Mother and her sisters: Aunt Dorothy Jo and Aunt Estelle.

Left to right: Papa, me, Stella, Mother, Cassie, and Floyd.

$\mathcal{W}$e rarely went to church on Easter for it was usually before new shoes had been bought for all of us and overalls for the boys, and before Mother had made new shirts and dresses. But we'd go on a picnic. Mother would fill a brown paper poke with the eggs we'd colored, and she'd pack a box of fried chicken, potato cakes, biscuits, and cinnamon rolls for the lunch. Papa carried the food high upon his shoulders so we couldn't eat it up too soon.

The Easter eggs were colored with dyes made from onion skins for yellow, oak bark for orange, and walnut hulls for brown. We left some of the eggs white. Later, when we used food coloring, we had more colors, but the ones Mother made stand out in my memory and are my favorites.

After we ate our picnic lunch, we'd have an egg fight. This game was simple. One of us would hold an egg in our fist, then someone else would tap it with their egg until one broke. The winner got the cracked egg. Whoever ended up with the most eggs was the winner. The boys usually won because the girls would pick the pretty light-colored ones that were the white-shelled eggs. The boys always chose the tiny bantam eggs or the brown eggs that the red chickens laid. They knew those eggs were tougher.

There is no prettier place on earth to hide Easter eggs than in the woods, hills, and valleys where we lived. We waded in flowers everywhere we went. Spring glowers of all kinds—red, blue, white, yellow, pink, and lavender—grew as if God Himself had walked along and put them where He knew we'd be. The only places they didn't grow were the lanes made by the cattle or in the sled roads. But we didn't like to walk there, anyway; we preferred the fields and creeks.

Stella was born in late spring. She had blonde hair like Papa and big brown eyes like Mother. But she was natural like Papa, so sure of life and her own ability. She is smart and learns everything quickly. Lots of times Stella and I insist we remember something, but Mother and Papa will say that we couldn't remember, because we were just babies when it happened. So now we tell them we even remember being born. Sometimes Stella almost convinces me that she does. Of course, it's because we've been told the stories so many times.

*P*apa said the time he came home from work and found David and Denver in the field with the killer mule was the first time he almost had a heart attack. Papa has had a heart condition for years, and he takes medicine every day. But he says that day was the first time he really knew he had a heart condition. He used to buy and trade livestock a lot, trying to make a little extra money. He wasn't buying prime livestock, just animals to trade on and hopefully make a few dollars. This mule was latched in the stable until he could get him to market. He had an extra bar on the door for safety. Nobody remembers if the boys knew the mule was dangerous.

Papa was walking to the house from the main road where his ride had dropped him off when he saw David, Denver, and the mule in the middle of the field. Papa started running toward them. Reaching for the plow lines, he

Front row (left to right): Randy and Floyd. *Back row (left to right):* Bobby, David, Denver, and Papa.

said, "Boys, what on earth are you doing?" They told him, "We're working, Papa. See, we have taken all the rocks out of this field today." Sure enough, they had. They had a rock wall started at the edge of the field and the sled full of rocks when he got to them. He said the mule didn't pay any more attention to them than he would have to a horse fly. Papa swears the mule looked around at him as if to say, "Are you stupid?" The mule was so wild that Papa almost didn't get him out of his gears and unhooked from the trace chains. Papa nailed the barn door shut until he could get the mule to market that weekend. He said he thought he was going to have to sell him with the gears on. He was that dangerous. Someone had surely treated him bad, for him to fear and hate humans so. Papa asked the boys how they got the gears on the mule. They said that Denver climbed up on top of the stable door and just dropped them on and he didn't kick at them when they hooked him to the sled.

This makes me think how wonderful this world would be if we all could treat every living creature, human and animal, with respect and dignity. We may never have a perfect world, but if all our teachers—and each of us is truly a teacher—could help us learn gentleness and a kinder way, we could have a more beautiful world than we have today.

*A*nyone who has ever lived on a farm knows well that at some time you'll own a dog, cat, cow, horse, goat, or something that acts stupid. Ours was a chicken named Penny. Penny was a long-legged, ugly red hen. But the kids liked her and thought she was funny. Lord, she was ugly! Even our roosters didn't like her. If you dropped anything, Penny grabbed it and ran. It didn't matter what it was as long as she could get hold of it somewhere with her beak, and she'd run with it all day.

Rachel, who was the baby, was playing in the yard with her bottle. After she emptied out the milk, she pulled the nipple off. Penny grabbed it and ran. We panicked! There wasn't another nipple in the house! Rachel had bitten the ends out of all the rest. She was old enough not to have a bottle, but she still wanted one, so she had one. She got terribly upset without her bottle. Penny ran all around the yard. We threw sticks and rocks at her, but she would not drop the nipple! Everybody had skinned places and bruises where they had fallen. Dolly carries the scar on her knee today from getting cut while chasing Penny.

Our beautiful mother and her younger brothers.

*O*ne spring, when Randy was a teenager, he was fortunate to be able to purchase a beautiful red rooster from Sam Ellis, who was selling all his roosters. Randy named this rooster Señor Tuffass. Of course, we just called him by his first name when Mother and Papa were around.

And Señor was tough! When Randy wasn't fighting the poor rooster, he was trying to breed him to a prize hen to produce more roosters of equal quality. After a hard day, Randy and Bobby sometimes let Señor get drunk by giving him sips of whiskey in a teaspoon.

Because of an argument over Señor Tuffass and another boy's gamecock, Randy and a neighbor boy decided to settle the whole thing by fighting each other. Randy didn't really want to fight this boy, and anyway, he didn't have on his fighting boots. So, to delay the action, he sent Floyd home to get the boots.

It was a lengthy delay, since the house was a mile away. Randy and the boy just sat down and waited for Floyd to return with the boots. As soon as he pulled the boots on, they had their fight. Floyd recalls, "I should've just whipped the boy for Randy, like I usually had to do. It would've been over quicker, and I wouldn't have had to walk two miles."

Señor Tuffass died an honorable death in the pits, while fighting a younger rooster. But I really think he died from exhaustion, brought on by fighting and fathering.

Our only picture of Señor Tuffass.

Dolly and her brothers. *Left to right:* Bobby, Randy, Floyd, David, and Denver.

$\mathcal{P}$apa is a real prankster. Not long ago he was sitting on his porch when a carload of good ole boys, who were somewhat stewed, asked him if they could ride the bull in the field near the house. Papa told them he didn't care a bit. Evidently, the bull cared. One of the boys got on him and the bull tossed him off; another one would climb on, only to be immediately thrown off. This sequence continued for quite some time, accompanied by enthusiastic cheering. The man who owned the field and the bull came driving up and demanded to know what they were doing. "Riding this bull," they replied. "And Lee said he didn't care." The neighbor said, "I don't guess he does; it's not his bull, it's mine!"

Trading was a source of fun as well as a necessity to supplement the income of families. Papa had dealings with an old trader who'd cheated him a couple of times, but Papa bided his time and retaliated.

Papa had a fine-looking, yellow-eyed dog. The old trader was impressed with the dog and wanted to buy it from Papa. In the course of conversation, the trader asked Papa, "Does that dog like squirrels?" Papa told him, "Likes them better than any dog I've ever seen." So the trader took Papa's word and bought the yellow-eyed dog for a good price. A couple of weeks went by before the trader came back, bringing the dog with him. Papa was expecting him. "Lee, I've brought your dog home. He's gun shy. He won't go squirrel hunting with me, and you told me he liked squirrels." Papa grinned and said, "He does like squirrels, Lloyd, but you have to cook them for him first."

When Dolly came to visit one weekend in 1967, she was wearing a pink blouse and pink shorts. She stood near the edge of the porch, holding onto the post. Her husband, Carl Dean, kept hugging her and telling her how pretty she was in shorts. She said, "Carl, you're going to make me fall off the porch and get killed." He pulled her down on his lap and said, "No, baby, I'm not. I've decided to keep you."

Dolly was eating an apple when she told us about her contract with Porter Wagoner and her new job. She was pleased and told us she would be working a lot and that this might be her last trip to Sevierville for a while. She threw the apple core out in the yard. I later covered it with dirt and now it's a small tree, bearing fruit. After a very successful seven years for both Porter and Dolly, they went their separate ways, pursuing different goals.

Years later Dolly was appearing in concert at the Knoxville Coliseum. I had taken an unusual bouquet to her backstage and told her its story. Earlier that

Dolly and Porter.

evening, I had picked red roses and small branches off the apple tree. I had started the rosebushes from the cut flowers she'd sent me over the years. When they were ready to throw away, I couldn't do it, so I'd stick them in the damp dirt near the creek. The red roses took root and I transplanted them. The apple tree was the one started from the seeds of the apple Dolly was eating when she told me about her signing with Porter. It had tiny green apples on it for the first time that year, and there were still a few blossoms along with the apples.

The coliseum was completely full. I followed the usher down to the seat Dolly had reserved for me.

Dolly's high school graduation. *Front row (left to right):* Randy and Floyd. *Second row:* Freida and Rachel. *Back row (left to right):* me, Stella, Cassie, Dolly, Grandpa Jake, and Mother.

Tompall Glazer was the opening act, and he was almost through when I sat down. But I was impatient. I'd come to see my sister.

I sat waiting for Dolly to appear on stage; Tompall was through, and the music to "Higher and Higher" was becoming almost unbearable because of the anticipation. Then the spotlight suddenly flashed on and there she was . . . my beautiful sister!

I had seen Dolly perform before, but somehow this was a special night. Maybe I was tuned in to the audience, or more aware of how far she'd come—I don't know. Or maybe I was, for the first time, drawn away from being her sister into being one of the audience.

She led the audience from emotion to emotion as surely as if she had led them by the hand. "Coat of Many Colors" became as real to the audience as if each person were seeing the little girl's hurt and hearing the taunts and laughter. I looked around, and not only were the women and children crying, but also the men.

I looked at Dolly and remembered the baccalaureate of 1964 at the First Baptist Church in Sevierville. Each senior told what he or she planned to do in life. Some of the students planned to become nurses, doctors, teachers, and so on. Then it was Dolly's turn.

Dolly's senior picture.

Our family had seats near the middle of the church and we all leaned forward as Dolly stood up. Her voice carried clearly across the church auditorium. "I'm going to Nashville to be a singer and a songwriter." There was complete silence for a few seconds. Then there was a smattering of smothered laughter.

"I'm going to Nashville to be a singer and a songwriter." A big dream for a little girl. But it was no dream to us because Dolly had always made it clear to us that this was to be her destiny. No doubts, no second thoughts. She knew it was to be, and our family knew, too. Music has always been Dolly's love, almost a living companion to her. I've seen her forget all else to give herself to its bidding.

She sometimes wakes up in the middle of the night to write down the lyrics to a melody that comes through in a dream. She will suffer for days trying to capture an elusive melody that won't be still.

Other songs are written in crowds, for they cannot wait. Dolly will stop whatever she's doing and write her song on whatever she can find—a napkin, scrap of paper, or her hands. "The Seeker" was written in a matter of ten minutes or so. She just said to her secretary, "Judy, write this down." It was as if she were only the voice used to relay the message. She has said that this was one of the most profound religious experiences she has ever had.

The morning after Dolly's graduation, we all gathered at Mother's house to see Dolly before she left for Nashville. She was going to live with Uncle Bill Owens and his family. All of the kids were sitting around as Dolly finished putting on her makeup. She changed into a pretty dress with long sleeves and a white collar.

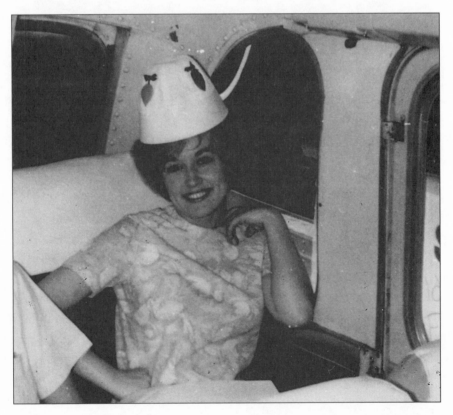

Dolly on her senior trip.

Dolly being presented a plaque honoring the Dolly Parton Scholarship Fund at Sevier County High School. Presenting the plaque is Paul Bogart, the late superintendent of schools.

We wanted her to go but it was so hard for us to be unselfish and give her up. The ones of us who had married had stayed in the community. This was the first time any of us had left home except for the time David had spent in the Marine Corps.

A house feels so empty when someone you love leaves. We counted the hours we knew it would take her to get to Nashville. The little ones would ask, "Is she there yet?" And we would look at the clock and tell them how much longer.

Finally, Mother looked at the clock and announced, "Dolly's getting off the bus now." What we didn't know was that within hours she would be waving to the man who would become her husband.

Carl Dean was doing what most boys did, driving around, looking for pretty girls. Dolly was walking down the street. She was in the town where she knew she belonged. She was eighteen, just out of high school, and on her own. Her independence was sweet and she knew that Nashville was the door to her new life. When the boy waved at her, she did what she had always done—she waved back.

In the area where we were born and raised, everybody waves or "throws up" his hand when someone passes by in a car or on foot. We've always done it, and we still do. Carl swears that his arm gets so tired from waving at people when he visits Sevier County that he is going to have an artificial arm attached to his car. Then all he will have to do is push a button and the arm will fly up to greet all the neighbors who wave when he passes.

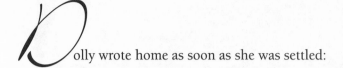olly wrote home as soon as she was settled:

Dear Mama and Daddy,

I hope this letter finds everybody well and happy. As for me, I'm fine I guess. I'm just a little lonesome and a whole lot homesick. I got to Nashville alright and I thought I'd better write and let you know 'cause I knew you'd be worried about me. I don't want you to be worried about me 'cause I'm going to be all right once I get settled and used to being away from home.

I didn't realize how much I loved you and all them noisy kids until I left. I didn't realize how hard it was to leave home, either, until I started to leave and everybody started crying, including me. I cried almost all the way to Nashville. I wanted to turn around a few times and come back. But you know how I've always wanted to go to Nashville and be a singer and songwriter. And I believe I'll make it if I try long and hard enough. Someday I'll make it!

Don't worry about trying to send me any money or anything because I got a job singing on an early morning TV show called the *Eddie Hill Show*. A couple of folks already told me they might record a couple of my songs so I'll be making enough money to get by. I don't want you to be worrying about me being hungry or anything.

Nashville's not exactly what I thought it was. I'm going to like it once I get used to it. And I don't want you to be worrying about me getting in trouble either 'cause I'll be good just like I promised you I would when I left.

Well, I can't think of anything else to say. I guess I'd better close for now. You write me real soon 'cause I'll be real anxious to hear from you.

Tell everybody I said hello 'cause I sure miss you and love you an awful lot.

With love as always,

Dolly

One of my favorite pictures of Dolly.

Uncle Bill Owens is a singer and songwriter, and he was Dolly's manager. She worked doing shows with him and rented a trailer from him. She did demo tapes, worked at odd jobs, and babysat. She pounded the streets, knocking on the doors of the vast, complex music business.

She and Uncle Bill traveled to shows all over Tennessee and to the surrounding states in his old car. They never knew if the car was going to get there or break down on the road. Many times Dolly wrapped herself in a quilt because the car had no heater and cold air poured in through the holes that had rusted through the floorboard.

They always packed sandwiches and a thermos of coffee and fruit jars filled with tea, because they couldn't afford to buy food at a restaurant. Dolly would have to shift her position in the seat each time a bump in the road brought a new spring through the upholstery.

When Dolly moved into an apartment by herself, we had a new source of worry. I could see all kinds of sadists and perverts lurking outside her windows. So I included in the sewing box I had fixed for her a hammer, nails, and a note instructing her to nail her windows shut so no one could open them from the outside. Later I learned she had done exactly as I told her and nailed shut all the windows in her second-story apartment. I've often wondered what the next tenant thought!

*C*arl was becoming more and more intrigued with our pretty, bubbly sister, and she with him. When she came home it was "Carl this," and "Carl that." She glowed when she told us of times she had visited his family. But mostly she talked of what she was doing and the songs she had written. We were the ones she sang her new songs to.

She'd tell us how she missed us, but we wouldn't hear about the many nights she cried until years later, when she could finally talk about it. It must have been terrible, for she had always had a house full of people to love, to fight with, and just to be a part of. How could we know that feeling? We still had each other.

Throughout this time, Carl was there, worrying about her and checking on her almost every day. Yet even he didn't know about the times she went hungry.

Dolly in her prom dress with Papa, who was going to church not the prom.

She came home one time and she might have weighed ninety pounds. It scared us to death! But she told us she had been dieting. When we asked her how she could lose that much weight so quickly, she said, "It wasn't easy!" Later we learned that she had so little to eat and so much pride that she almost starved. After that, she went back to Nashville loaded down with home-canned foods and meal and flour to make bread.

Years later we asked her why she didn't ask Papa to send her some money. She said, "I was afraid he would send me money all right . . . but to come home with!"

Dolly and Carl dated when she was not on the road or working. They were in love and planned to

Papa and Dolly in more casual dress.

marry. Mother and some of the children had already met him. In April 1966 Dolly brought Carl home to meet the rest of the family.

We gave her a bridal shower with just a few girlfriends and a lot of family. It was held at my house. We decorated the living room and kitchen in pink and white. The centerpiece for the table included pink and white carnations and the table in the living room had a pink-and-white parasol surrounded by gifts.

The day before Carl and Dolly got to our house, I had bought my son, Mitchell, two colored Easter chicks and two baby ducks from our local Temple Milling Company. We had put the chicks in a shoebox and had the ducks in the bathtub lined with newspapers. Where else do you keep baby ducks? Temple's must not have had rabbits that Easter or we would have had rabbits hopping around the house, too.

Dolly and Mitchell had to play with the chicks and ducks, and when they left them alone, of course they cheeped louder and louder, wanting more attention. Carl never commented but he sent funny looks toward the bathroom now and then.

I had seen a snapshot of Carl before meeting him and, of course, Dolly had told me about him. I was a little leery of meeting the "perfect man." He is handsome, very tall, with dark brown hair and eyes. He is tolerant, open-minded, patient, sensitive. He has a sarcastic sense of humor that all of us enjoy. When Dolly and I were alone, she said, "Isn't he the best-looking man you have ever seen?"

Carl says he never lived until he met Dolly. On Memorial Day 1966 Carl and Dolly were married in Ringgold, Georgia, in the presence of Mother. We've

Carl Dean, Dolly's husband.

Carl at a "Dolly Day" in Sevierville.

still not figured out why Mother went with them. She may have wanted to attend the wedding, or she may have convinced them that they would need her to sign the papers for Dolly.

They were married in a church, and after the ceremony they had driven almost back to Nashville when Mother realized that she had left her purse in the church! Now Mother's pocketbook is a legend. It's like a drugstore, variety store, hardware store, and filing cabinet all rolled into one. It contains more telephone numbers than the Nashville directory, from former attorney general David Pack's to the president's. And it's heavier than a steamer trunk. Without it she's lost, she can't function, can't cope. For some people a purse is a convenience; for Mother, it's security.

There was nothing Carl could do but go all the way back to Ringgold and retrieve it from the bench where she had set it down when she took their picture. So Dolly and Carl ended up spending most of their wedding night with Mother!

*D*olly wrote me this letter later in the year:

Hello Willadeene and Arthur and, of course, Mitchell,

Well, I've been wanting to write you for a long time but I never have the time to write.

Mama said you moved and quit working. I'll bet that went over real big with Mitchell, didn't it? I talked to Mama this morning and she said you thought you might go back to work. I hope you don't. You don't need to be working on a job. If you work then I can't come and stay a week with you. See! No really don't get mad at me for saying this, but Mitchell will be in school next year and you'll be away from him all the time. So I'd stay home until he started to school, then I'd go to work if I wanted to. Well, it isn't any of my business anyway and that's a poor excuse for saying, "I want you to stay home so I can come to see you," isn't it? Oh, well.

Dolly in a Sevier County concert.

My "Dumb Blonde" made top 10 nationwide. I'm cutting an album this week. It will be called *Hello, I'm Dolly*, so it will be like *Hello, Dolly*. That's cute, don't you think? It features "Dumb Blonde." It will be out in about a month, I'll send you one.

My new record will be out next week. It's called "Something Fishy." I wrote it myself, too. It's real good. I have been working my tail off. I stay gone on the road all the time now. I did the *Bill Anderson Show* two weeks ago. Do you get it up there? It will be shown in a week or two. I did four songs on it. It turned out real good. I didn't get a chance to send Mitchell a card from Canada. That's where we filmed it.

I hope we get to come sometime this month. We plan to come every weekend and then we have to work. I like it, though.

I wrote Lenore and Hulet a letter to thank him for that family board he made. I sure took a long time about doing it, but I thought

Carl with Dolly at the ceremony where Dolly received an award for "Put It Off Until Tomorrow," in 1966.

we were going home every week. How do you like your new house? Carl really liked it down there. I do, too. Who bought your other house?

Carl is working all the time now. We hardly ever see each other it seems like. I want to come home and a stay a week before long. I'll keep the car. I've got my license now. We'll do some things.

I'll probably do another album off of "Something Fishy" and I want to put that song of yours ("He Loves Me Not") on it. I have a new record coming out by Hank Williams, Jr., that I wrote myself. It's called "I'm in No Condition." It is supposed to be out this week so listen for it. (I didn't write Kitty Wells' song she has out now "Love Makes the World Go Around." The one we wrote is called "More Love Than Sense." It will be out later.) "Fuel to the Flame" is No. 7 nationwide. We're doing real good, finally!

Well, tell Mitchell I wrote Darrell and I told him I would tell Mitchell I wrote him a letter. Tell Mitchell I'll write him postcards every time I can when I travel.

I love you,
Dolly

The bond between child and grandparent is one of the strongest, I believe. I know it was my grandpa Jake Owens who was the first male I learned to depend on, respect, and love, since my mother and I lived in his home until I was old enough to walk and talk. All his life I was never far away from him.

Grandpa was a part-time school teacher and a music teacher. After Grandpa and Grandma Rena were married he felt there was a different kind of teaching the Lord wanted him to do. He studied his Bible diligently and attended Bible College and most of all he prayed for guidance in his life.

Grandpa and Grandma moved a lot when the family was young. The first thing Grandpa had to do when they moved into a new house was build shelves. Then Grandma would unpack her pretty things, figurines, vases, her carnival glass and ruby red dishes, cut-glass bowls, and a cookie jar made in the shape of a bear. Grandma loved a pretty home and flowers, but she was always having to move and leave the flowers she had planted before she could see them bloom.

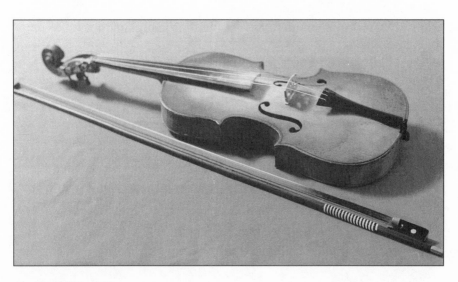

Grandpa Jake's violin.

An old picture of me just fiddling around.

Grandpa Jake reading his Bible.

The first things Grandpa packed were what he considered most valuable, the Bible, family pictures, and the violin. This violin has been in our family for more than a hundred years and is reported to be a violin of exceptional quality. Uncle Frank Messer was given the violin when he was nineteen as payment for building a small frame house for his father, Isaac Messer.

At one time the violin had belonged to Grandpa Jake's great-grandfather, Solomon Grooms. The story goes that Solomon was walking across the mountains with his two grandsons John and Sol Sutton to visit their family in North Carolina. They met a band of vigilantes on top of Chestnut Mountain. Solomon was a union man and the vigilantes didn't like union men. They kept their guns pointed at Solomon and told him to play his favorite tune on his fiddle for them. As he played "Morgan's Retreat," they shot and killed him. The killers didn't harm the terrified grandsons. After the band of men rode off, Sol and John took the violin with them and ran the twenty miles home with the tragic news.

The violin was passed about among the Owens, Grooms, and Sutton families until Grandpa Jake Owens bought it from Frank Messer. Grandpa Jake told me this story. Then he told me the violin would belong to me because I was the eldest grandchild. I will cherish its memory always and will pass its history down to our descendants.

*A*t one time, almost every house had one or several religious posters made of heavy cardboard on their walls. These posters were always a deep, rich shade of purple, blue, red, or green. The words and pictures were made of silver glitter. School children sold them, and so did a lot of the churches, for twenty-five cents each. Almost everyone had several. They were almost as popular as the fans the funeral homes provided at funerals or revivals in the churches. My mother's brothers sold them as well as Cloverine and Rosebud salves.

The Grit paper was the first paper I ever read, and I still subscribe to it. They used to deliver the papers using a large bag of some sort that had the word *Grit* written on it. It was and is a newsy little paper. Even Uncle Alden got to sell these wonderful things, because he had a bike and could ride. I didn't have a bike and couldn't ride, anyway. Only boys were allowed to sell *The Grit* paper. They sold boxes of coconut candy bars, large flat ones that had rainbow stripes. I still buy a smaller version now but they don't taste as good as they did when one of my uncles would open one bar and we all got a taste.

When plastic curtains first came to the dime store, everybody had to have plastic curtains. There were countless designs and colors to choose from. They were cheap and we didn't have to wash them. The strong odor of plastic stayed in the house for weeks. But we were so proud when we got the new curtains. And we would be happy when we got new linoleum for our floors. We liked it, like the smell of a new car. When I was growing up, we never went to town to buy linoleum but bought it off a truck that came through sometimes twice a year. We waxed the linoleum with Johnson's paste wax. When it dried we'd use an old worn-out quilt or bedspread to buff and make it shine.

Sometimes in the thirties, Mother remembers, you could buy handmade mattresses from a traveling salesman driving a truck. Wallpaper was another luxury people enjoyed. We had to order it from catalogs and wait impatiently until it came. The wallpaper we got was always thick and heavy, almost like a thin poster or extra heavy construction paper. The pattern that I remember best was the big red roses on a cream-colored background. We sometimes used paste to put our wallpaper up with and we sometimes used special tacks with gold washers.

Many of us seem to need to create some of these old memories even now. Often we will decorate one or two rooms with all the things we used to have such as old-fashioned wallpaper and linoleum. Dolly has several houses and some of them are what we call "memory houses," where she has had the whole dwelling decorated in the old ways. When we get together at one of these homes, and we often do, it is very comforting to us to be able to go through the door and step back to the good old days, if only for a few hours.

A PR picture from early Nashville days.

Randy had always wanted a pony. One of our neighbors gave Randy an old cat with a couple of kittens. It wasn't a pony but it was something.

Floyd wanted one of the kittens but Randy wouldn't give him one. So Floyd asked Mother just where the cat got the kittens. Instead of sitting down with him and explaining, Mother just kept on doing whatever she was doing and said, "She probably dug them up in the woods."

Floyd watched that cat's every move until finally he saw her run into the woods. He saw her digging and pushed her aside figuring he could finish digging up his own kittens. It didn't take him long to figure out she wasn't digging up kittens but covering up what we all know cats cover up, but it was too late.

It took Floyd quite a while to get over that and a while longer to even like cats again. Even now if we see a cat near him, one of us will say, "Are you sure you don't want to follow that cat, Floyd?"

Several years ago, Dolly bought Mother the first of her many cars. We all just about had heart attacks and nervous breakdowns while she learned to drive—all of us, that is, except Dolly. She just went back to Nashville, telling Mother she was giving her her freedom.

Dolly also bought Mother several pantsuits. Some were red, some green, and some yellow. Mother had never worn pants. It wasn't long after that that Mother stopped dipping snuff and started smoking cigarettes instead.

One Sunday when we were all home, Papa took several of us aside and told us that he was worried about Mother and that he wasn't so sure she was all right. Sometimes, he said, she didn't have his supper ready until six or seven o'clock! She had been gone all day in her new car and just quarreled at him if he said anything to her about it.

We assured him that she was indeed all right. Now we tell them that for the first years of their life we were sorry for Mother because Papa's word was the law, and the last years we were sorry for Papa because Mother keeps breaking the law!

This is a piece Maw Taylor wrote remembering spring days and happy times. Her writing is precious to me and I still miss her. She died in November of 1995.

You want to know about my friend Miss Amy (Willadeene). If you'll come along with me, my pencil and paper, we'll take a little trip down memory lane.

I lived with her and her then invalid husband, Raymond, for several years. When he died, I thought I'd be leaving, that she wouldn't need me anymore. She asked me not to leave so I stayed on.

Let me share part of the years with you. I couldn't believe there could be this kind of person in such a cruel, rough world as we live in today. Always kind, caring, giving, all of the Partons are givers not takers.

Her son is just like her. I tease him and my son, David, saying, put a dress on you two and you'd be just like your mothers. They look and act like us, Mitchell like her, David like me.

The doctor has told me that I am dying with cancer, with only a short time to live. I always told Miss Amy that I hoped I'd have someone like her to take care of me when it was my time. Guess what! She is with me. When I feel good we talk about olden times. I wrote a little booklet called *My Experiences While Living with the Parton Family.*

It was like going through a tunnel, living with the Parton family all those years. The uncertainty of each new day and what it would bring was always quite an experience. The first time I met Miss Amy I thought anybody that beautiful couldn't be hard to work for, and she looked like she had just walked out of charm school. Boy did I get my bubble burst the first time I stayed overnight. I saw "Miss Charm" in her pajamas, no makeup on and barefooted. She could have been in the children's storybooks I've read. I've seen people that looked like her on *Little House on the Prairie* and *The Waltons.* After that I kind of knew I was in the right place.

My duties were to do two things: help to take care of her invalid husband and keep the house clean. That didn't seem hard. After all, I'd been to college and had raised a family. Well hold on to your hat! Those two things I accepted with pleasure, but I inherited some extra jobs: telephone receptionist, go-for (go for this and go for that), animal trainer, pooper scooper, chief of the lost-

and-found department, baby-sitter (infants to elderly). I had never seen so many animals and children. "Children" meant grandchildren, nieces, nephews, brothers, sisters. I also did things for Mr. and Mrs. Parton. I also took care of the dogs and cats that stayed in the house: Saatchi, Missy (almost blind and very old), Max, a large Doberman, and Sex the Siamese cat, beautiful but aggravating.

Regina "Maw" Taylor and me.

When I met each of the Parton girls, I said to myself, "They can't all be that pretty," but they are. The boys are all so handsome, it makes me wish I was young again. Wouldn't my old friends from Virginia be surprised to know that I live in the house with a bunch of Partons, all the time making coffee for none other than Dolly and her husband, Carl. And also helping take care of Freida and her sweet daughter Jada.

When Saatchi had been to the groomer's, she'd act like I was nobody. For days her nose would be in the air, as though she were saying: "Don't tell me what to do, Maw." Now you'd have to be around this dog for a while to know what I'm talking about. When she goes to bed, she has to be completely covered with a blanket, like a person who has the covers up to their neck. I know this sounds crazy, but it's true. Working for Miss Amy got more interesting every day.

Sex, the cat, lied once. She broke a globe on an old oil lamp and marched off as pretty as you please. When Miss Amy asked about it, I told her Sex broke it. She acted like she didn't believe me. Shortly thereafter we went shopping. She told the store owner that I or the cat had lied. I said the cat did it, and the cat had obviously told her I did it. Max and Missy just mostly minded their own business. I have never been a pet lover, but I did learn to like these four critters.

When I first went there to work she had told me when I answered the phone to say, Buzzeo residence, their last name, and ask who was calling. That didn't seem too hard. So when the phone rang I'd say, "Bozeo residence," and "Who's calling please?" trying to act real uptownish. Now Buzzeo certainly isn't a hard word to say, but somewhere in the back of my mind Bozeo computed, and it would just pop out.

Well, my boss lady called home one day, and I answered my usual way. She said, "Maw, the next time you answer the phone please just say hello." That pleased me a lot, for I'm not much into foreign languages and difficult names.

Well, I hope I haven't bored you too much, time is moving on, and I need a nap first. I probably won't get any rest, because I'll be dreaming of being at Miss Amy's house—the dogs barking, buzzers going off, the door bell ringing, and the phone ringing all at the same time. I'll have the phone in one hand and the door knob in the other, and wake up.

~

Papa and all of our brothers went on vacation with us in the early 1980s. We traveled in Dolly's new custom-made Golden Eagle bus. Terry, Dolly's driver, was the only one who wasn't a family member. It had required quite a lot of persuasion to get the boys to take off work and to get Bobby to fly here from Washington. It was Dolly's idea and my job was to get everyone to go along, not an easy task.

Freida had been sick for months, from a fall. She had just moved to New York and finished a rock album. She had fallen down a flight of stairs and was still using a walker and brace; however, she's a trouper and she was going because everyone else was.

Dolly, Randy, and Stella had just discovered they had to be in Las Vegas and then in Los Angeles before the week was over. Rachel had to be in Los Angeles to start the filming of the TV version of *Nine to Five*. So the first thing we did was cut our vacation in half.

Bobby, Floyd, Dolly, and Stella were all on the bus when I got there. I'd fixed a picnic lunch. Cassie got on the bus asking us to guess what she'd brought to eat. We couldn't. She had gotten an old recipe for chocolate oatmeal cookies from a woman who used to cook at Caton's Chapel School. All of my cooking was then forgotten, as we begged and pleaded for the cookies. We even went so far as trying to buy them from her. Someone threatened her and then finally just took them. Freida had just been to the doctor, and Mark Anderson, her husband, kept running around trying to get her settled with all her things on board the bus. All she wanted was her earphones and rock music so she could tune us out. We made room for her on the couch and Mark kept fussing over her. I can't believe that Mark and Papa never figured out that you can't tell Mother and Freida anything. They always do just as they please anyway.

Everybody told jokes except me. They won't let me tell any because I forget the punch lines and drive them crazy.

We camped in parks, we cooked out, we went shopping, we sang at the campfire, and we fussed. Papa got so nervous and finally mad because we couldn't agree on anything. No one can imagine, except Mother and Papa, what it is like to be cooped up with eleven bickering adult children.

We found the smallest church I have ever seen. We tried to get Mother and Papa to go there and renew their marriage vows so we could all watch, but they just laughed and told us they wanted to mean it the next time.

We spent a day and night on the beach. We were still bickering and being childish. Dolly told us she planned this trip so she could get to know and see what made each one of us tick. Well, believe me, it was even more enlightening than anticipated—for me, anyway! We took long walks on the beach with different members of the family and sometimes had long serious talks. In the afternoon Mother and Papa went for a walk by themselves. We yelled and whistled at them from the balcony of the motel. We had everyone on the beach looking and enjoying the razzing we were giving our parents. They were so embarrassed and tried to act like they didn't hear us as they almost ran down the beach.

We spent the afternoon playing. We had footraces and we built sand castles and we argued.

The last night of our trip was my birthday, so we decided to party. We started real early. When the more sensible ones of us decided it was time to go to bed, I wasn't allowed to because it was *my birthday* we were celebrating. One thing about us, we'll celebrate anything—a new hat, an old hat, the weather—and we'll celebrate just because. . . .

Papa, Randy, Denver, Bobby, Floyd, and David on a family trip to Myrtle Beach,

We went to the nearest club to wind up our night. Freida can be a real charmer when she wants to be. She persuaded us that she could do anything the rest of us could, except dance. We closed the place at two A.M.

No one was sleepy except Bobby and me. We couldn't talk the rest of them into going to bed so we all sat at the pool for a while. Then everybody went upstairs to bed except Freida, Randy, and Denver. They were pretty loud and had been asked by the management to please quiet down. So Bobby and I came down one more time and tried to get them to go to their rooms. We got to the bottom of the stairs and heard Freida yelling. A small crowd, including policemen, had gathered around her, but Randy and Denver were nowhere to be seen. We finally understood what she was yelling about. Somebody had hit her! Well, now we were mad. Bobby and I were outraged that anyone would hit our poor sister who couldn't even walk without a walker.

We asked everybody if they saw who hit Freida and Freida pointed to a chair on the other side of the pool. There sat Randy with his head in his hands. About this time Denver came from behind the building, not knowing what had happened any more than the rest of us.

The police had us now. They threw Bobby, Randy, and Denver up against the wall. After a lot of questions and answers we figured out that Randy and Freida had really had a fight. Freida had hit Randy a few times with her walker, so he slapped her.

The police finally agreed to let Bobby and me take them to their rooms, but only after we promised not to let them out again that night. Mother and Papa didn't know what had happened; they'd slept through it all.

What a relief it was to be on our way back home. Everyone was so quiet. Randy was in a bunk with the curtains pulled down. Freida was in the back of the bus with the door closed.

After we left Mother and Papa at their home in Sevierville, we asked Randy what had happened between Freida and him. He said, "I was just trying to give her some good advice." We all laughed at him and told him, "Now, you know what people think of your advice." Freida and Randy apologized to each other, and most of us were grateful that particular vacation was over.

Now, when we are cutting up and telling things we did as kids, Papa tells us he had no idea how much trouble we got into as children. I guess he and Mother don't realize we still fuss and fight and get into trouble even to this day.

One night, our husbands, Carl, Larry, Carroll, and Arthur, went out on the town. No, we wives weren't invited, which was a relief, because we've lived through a lot of hair-raising and extremely embarrassing stunts. After hitting most of the bars in Knoxville, they wound up at the Chatterbox, feeling no pain and acting tough.

Arthur knew the boys in the band, so they didn't argue with him when he borrowed a guitar and announced that he and Carl were going to entertain. Carl's voice rang out, doing justice to the first verse of "Branded Man." He stopped, turned to Arthur who was still playing, and said, "Hell, Arthur, that isn't what I'm singing." Arthur's serious look matched his voice. "I know, Carl, but 'Tom Dooley' is all I know how to play!" Their musical efforts, among other things, weren't appreciated by the bouncer, who threw them out the door.

As the bouncer was weaving them through the tables, Arthur leaned toward a table full of women and said to one of them, "Hi, good-looking!" And the lady shouted back, "Too bad I can't say the same about you!" Then without a moment's pause, Arthur retorted, "You could, if you'd lie like I did!" Carroll and Larry sneaked out, hoping no one would see them.

The Parton girls a long time ago. *Front row (left to right):* Cassie, Stella, Dolly, and me. *Second row (left to right):* Larry, Carroll (Stella's former husband), Carl, and Arthur (my former husband).

Carl and Arthur, in one last effort to be in the spotlight, told the club owner, "Buddy, our wives could buy this damn place." Unperturbed, he answered, "Buddy, they'd have to if you expect to sing here again or even come through this door!"

Fortunately the guys must have decided that this kind of behavior was immature. Or maybe Larry and Carroll wouldn't go with them anymore, so they started doing only those things all four of them could enjoy. I don't remember them ever doing anything outrageous again.

The jail of Sevier County was not known as a place of leisure for the men and boys who were assigned there by our judge. Every day they were loaded up in an old Fleetwood Coffee delivery van and taken out to work on the roads and bridges. They were never called convicts or a chain gang (they weren't chained); they were just called the Fleetwood Coffee Boys. We kids thought they were fascinating and loved to catch sight of them going by in the truck.

David remembers a man known all over the county as Little Johnny Cricket. He drove a horse and buggy. The buggy was black and had one seat with a top over it. Johnny was small and spry and dressed in black. He made his living peddling fresh fruit. He was loved especially by the children who would run to meet him because he would always give them some of the cherries, plums, or peaches.

Summer

The rippling sound
of the water
over the worn and ragged rocks,
the fresh scent
of wild flowers
in the shady lane—
this spot is different from anyplace else
along the creek.
A breeze blows there
continually.
I love it.

Summer meant long days and chiggers; hard work in the fields and sweat bees; canning and drying food for the winter; and swimming, playing, and poison ivy.

Back on the first day of May, we kids had shed our undershirts and shoes, so by June our feet were tough and used to running over rocks and rough places. Our noses were sunburned and peeling, and our freckles were popping out everywhere.

Our day began at sunup. After breakfast, while the day was cool, we took our hoes to the field and followed Papa as he plowed the crops behind our chestnut workhorse, Old Bob. We chopped weeds and loosened the ground around each plant. When Papa plowed the first couple of times, we'd even have to uncover some of the plants. We worked all day long as he plowed the long cornfields and tobacco patches, the cane patch, the big garden, and the bean patch we tended. Later, we would sell the vegetables we didn't need.

I can still see Papa bending over the plow handles as he turned the dirt, his blue cotton shirt dark with sweat, the sleeves rolled up above his elbows. We would carry him water in quart jars. He would stop, lean on the plow, and push his hat back from his forehead as he surveyed what he had done or what we were doing. Papa's arms, face, and neck first would be sunburned, then darkly tanned later in the summer.

Papa's work boots.

We all worked. We wanted to at first, then we worked because we had to. We loved the smell of the freshly turned earth and the coolness of it on our bare feet. But as the summer wore on, we began to dread seeing Papa gear up the horse, for we knew very well where we'd spend the day.

Even today, I can remember the water we drank from the quart jar in the field. It had picked up the taste and smell of the rubber seal on the two-piece

Above: Cassie and Papa. Papa is working. Cassie is just getting a free ride.
Below: Papa on the job tying steel—one of many hard jobs he has done in his life.

jar lid. I remember the smell of the horse, the sweat and leather; the sound of the gear chains and swingletree as Papa said, "Get up, Bob. Gee, haw." ("Gee" meant right and "haw" meant left, so Papa didn't have to pull on the check lines.) Old Bob would work to the sound of Papa's directions.

Mother always dipped snuff, and in the summer if we got bee-stung, she would dab snuff on the spot to draw the poison out. It worked. A wet tobacco leaf will do the same thing. It also works on insect and spider bites. We knew exactly what to do when we got stung and we didn't hesitate to do it.

When the day's work was finished, as usual we would go to the creek and play and splash in the water until it was time for supper.

My brothers and sisters will enjoy teasing me about this picture, but I decided to use it anyway.

A family gathering. *Left to right:* Aunt Estelle, great-Aunt Sarah, cousin Mary Lou, great-Aunt Exa, great-Uncle Sandberry, and his wife, Aunt May.

*D*uring summer, we would sometimes go to church on Sunday, but sometimes we would have a picnic or go swimming, taking our inflated inner tubes with the big red patches. Dolly always wanted to play "baptizing," so we would. We must have baptized her at least fifty times every summer!

My brothers would slide down the creek bank into the water, sometimes on their backsides and sometimes on their stomachs. No matter how many times Mother washed their overalls, there always seemed to be some mud stains left in them.

We would pick daisies and pull off each petal saying, "He loves me, he loves me not." Then we'd crumble the centers and throw them up in the air to see how many we could catch (to see how many children we would have). Don't try this yourself, for we caught handfuls, and we only have one, two, or three children each.

We would sit on the creek banks with Mother, and she would help us make rings, bracelets, and necklaces from the reeds that grew there. She would sit for hours and help us braid and fasten the reeds.

We'd catch butterflies and we'd pull down beech and apple tree limbs to look at birds' nests. Sometimes we'd catch grasshoppers and watch them chew and spit their old brown juice. At the end of the day on the way home, we'd cut forked limbs for a pair of stilts, or "tommy walkers," which always blistered our feet and gave us stone bruises as we hobbled back to the house.

Left to right: Uncle Henry, Aunt Estelle, Uncle Louis, Mother, and Uncle Alden.

Freida, Rachel, and Floyd on a summer vacation.

Denver was born late one summer evening. Papa had been squirrel hunting earlier in the day. When he came home, Mother told him to go for the doctor. Papa went to Uncle Wesley, who had a car, and asked him to go get the doctor. Then Papa came back to stay with Mother. We were at Grandpa and Grandma Owens' house. Grandma Rena boiled water, lit the lamp, heated flatirons, and scorched pieces of cloth torn from a clean sheet. These were scorched to kill any germs so they could be used as a band to protect the baby's navel.

David and I were wide-eyed just knowing something was about to happen, but of course we were put in a back room so we couldn't see or hear what was going on—only enough to arouse our curiosity.

Rachel, the youngest, was also a summer baby. So was our brother Larry, who died just hours after birth. The twins, Freida and Floyd, were also born in the summer. Mother has always felt she was doubly blessed with the twins. The twins were premature, each weighing less than four pounds. Floyd stayed in the hospital two weeks longer than Freida. When Freida was brought home, Cassie claimed her, and Stella was to get Floyd. Cassie was well pleased with her "baby," but Stella had grown quite attached to Freida also.

Freida working at Dollywood.

Floyd on vacation in Las Vegas with Dolly.

The big day finally came when Floyd was brought home from the hospital. He cried a great deal and had lots of black hair that wouldn't lie down like Freida's did. Stella took one look at him and whispered to Cassie, "Will you swap babies with me?" Cassie said loudly and firmly, "No! Your baby is ugly. His nose is red and his hair stands up!" I'm happy to say he looked much better in a day or so.

The twins have always been close. They have a special bond of love between them. I guess all twins do. Once when they were two or three years old, Mother was sewing on her sewing machine. Freida kept sticking her finger in the wheel of the treadle machine. Floyd was stacking stovewood, making pens for his play animals. Mother finally had to spank Freida to make her stop her annoying antics. Floyd threw a stick of stovewood and hit Mother in the back, saying, "Don't you whip my Sissie!" So Mother had to spank him, too. When she spanked one of them, she usually had to spank the other one as well.

Today Freida and Floyd still take up for each other. They may not always agree, but we never know it. They work those things out in private. It really is Freida and Floyd "against the world."

All during the time Mother was pregnant with our brother Larry, she had a dread. I guess you would call it foreboding. Once she was washing clothes outside in the washtubs, perhaps thinking of nothing except the job she was doing. She heard a voice call her name and say, "Your baby will die and not live." She straightened up from the washtub and scrub board to wipe her hands on her apron. The words came again, more clearly, "Your baby will die and not live." Mother put both hands on her stomach, as if to protect her unborn child. Now she knew why she'd felt such dread. I don't know if Mother questioned God or if she just accepted it. Knowing Mother, I believe she prayed, questioned a little, and then accepted whatever God did, because she felt that God knew best.

In our family, Mother and Papa would "give" an expected baby to one of the older brothers or sisters. When that particular baby was born, the one it had been given to not only shared in the care of the baby but also felt a great responsibility for it. While Mother was pregnant with Larry, Dolly had asked her several times if this baby could be hers. Mother would only say, "I suppose so." During this pregnancy Mother almost died from spinal meningitis. She was in the hospital for weeks. Grandma Rena stayed with Mother, and Papa stayed when he could, between working and trying to look after us. Aunt Ora came to check on us almost every day; and if she couldn't, she would send Uncle Earl. Mother's fever rose so high that she had to be packed in ice. Even with that, she slipped into a coma. The doctors told Papa and Grandma Rena that there was no hope of recovery. Grandma Rena, as always, turned to God for help. She refused to accept the doctors' predictions, instead

Dolly in the graveyard at the graves of our brother Larry and our nephew Donnie David.

choosing to put her faith in the Bible: "Whatsoever ye shall ask in prayer, believing, ye shall receive."

Finally, Mother came home, weak but well. Then on July 4 Mother's labor pains began. She went back to the hospital and on July 5 Larry was born. When Papa came home from the hospital, we were all waiting for him. After our other brothers and sisters had been born, Papa would tease us for a while by refusing to answer us when we asked, "Is it a boy?" or "Is it a girl?" So we expected his teasing. But this time there was no happy smile on his face as he walked through the doorway. He told us, "It was a baby brother, but he didn't live long." Larry had been born with defective lungs and lived just a few hours. Our hearts were broken. No matter how many brothers and sisters there were already in our family, we looked forward to each new arrival.

Dolly in prayer at Carson-Newman College.

The doctor let Mother hold Larry for as long as she wanted to. And she and Papa sat in her room together until she was ready to let them take Larry from her arms. Atchley's Funeral Home came for his little body, and Papa followed the hearse from the hospital in Knoxville to the funeral home in Sevierville. After Papa chose the casket and clothes for Larry, he came home to us.

When the neighbors heard about Larry's death, the men gathered together and dug his grave. The women cooked and brought food to the house for the family. This southern custom is especially prevalent in Sevier County, and it's a tradition that I hope will continue forever, because it shows the caring and love we feel for each other.

It was a hot day, and the grasshoppers whirred through the stubble of sedge grass in the cemetery as we walked to the tiny grave. From a distance, a rain crow's mournful, plaintive cry called for rain. Mother didn't attend the funeral, because she was still in the hospital. But the rest of the family was there.

The undertaker opened the casket so we could all see Larry for the last time. I felt such a sadness because I'd never felt his warmth or examined his little fingers and toes. We'd never brushed his dark hair. We felt so cheated because he died, and we hadn't been able to let him know how much we loved and wanted him.

When Larry's casket was lowered into the grave, Papa turned and walked away, unable to watch. I can still see him walking down the hill, alone, with his hands in his pockets and his head bowed. He was gone for a long time before he came back to the house.

When Mother came home from the hospital, Papa began working on a headstone for Larry. When the concrete was almost set, Mother took a knife and carved the headstone, taking great pains to do it right. Papa finished the stone, and he and Mother took it to the grave one evening. They went alone. At the time I didn't realize that they were showing their love for Larry in the only way they could.

We all picked flowers and took them to his grave, but Dolly would go and sit for hours by the grave, because he was to have been "her" baby. Though Larry didn't live long, he is as much a part of our family as any one of us. Mother keeps his picture on the wall of her and Papa's room, and when we talk or think of our brothers and sisters, he is always included—Larry, the very special baby we never got to hold.

When each child was born, Mother would take the child to church and have it dedicated to God. This service consisted of the preacher anointing the child with oil and saying, "Lord, we dedicate this child to you. Take it and use it for your glory. Amen." In this dedication, it was stressed that the parents had the serious responsibility of the religious teaching and upbringing of the child. It was not only their obligation to the child, but also a promise to God. There were times when we lived so far from church that we couldn't go for a dedication service, so Grandpa Jake would come to our house and perform the ceremony.

Mother's prayer was always that she would live to see her children grown. God has answered her prayer. She dedicated every one of her children and grandchildren to God, in prayer, even before they were born.

Above left: Bobby as a baby. *Middle left (left to right):* Estelle, Dorothy Jo, and Mother. *Above right (left to right):* me, Dolly, Denver, and David. *Lower left (left to right):* Mother, Dorothy Jo, and Estelle. *Middle:* Dolly as a toddler with me. *Lower right:* Grandma Rena.

*D*eath has always been very real to us because we weren't told pretty stories to whitewash the inevitable or lessen the tragedy of loss. Death was not unfamiliar, and we were exposed to it quite young. Our parents took us to funerals, and when there was a death in the community, school would let out and the teachers would take the children to the church or the deceased's house for the funeral.

When Grandpap Valentine died, I went with the school to his house, where his body was being viewed. He died not long after the school year began, and it was still warm enough to go barefoot, which I did that day. The teacher lined up all the schoolchildren and we marched in rows to Grandpap Valentine's house. I remember the feel of the road on my bare feet, the warm powdery dust that felt like warm water when I stepped in it. The boards of the swinging bridge were cool to my feet after walking on the hot road.

We filed into the house one by one. It felt dark and cool to me. My teacher apparently did not realize Grandpap Valentine was my great-grandfather. She told me to sit with my classmates rather than with my cousins. I will never forget how lonely I felt being treated as though I were an outsider during this important time. But that was the only time that ever happened to me.

Even though we frequently have to confront death, especially in such a large family, we can always rely on the comfort of our relatives. No one ever has to walk alone, especially in hard times.

Papa and me. We are mixing up a little home brew.

A smiling Papa.

*P*apa recently told us about a terrible day from his childhood:

I always remember it like it was yesterday, a lazy summer afternoon, the jar flies were singing and every now and then the wind would create miniature dust devils in the dirt. A group of men were sitting on a neighbor's front porch playing cards and drinking moonshine. One man was losing, so he bet his pocket watch, and then he lost that, too. He left without saying anything. A little later, the man returned and said to the man who won his watch, "I want my watch." The other man told him, "I won it fair and square."

I was leaning on Poppy's leg with my elbow propped in his lap. I remember that the man who lost his watch pulled a gun and started shooting. Poppy shoved me behind him with his arm and stood up. Two men were lying on the floor. There was blood all around, running across the porch and dripping into the dusty yard. The man put the gun to Poppy's face and pulled the trigger twice—but the gun was empty.

Papa says this memory gives him chills even now. The Grandpa Parton we knew was always a quiet, Christian man. It is hard to visualize the young and reckless man that Grandpa must have been in his younger days.

Last June, as I started to make an apple pie, I recalled how much we all loved green apples when we were kids. We knew better, but sometimes we would eat them anyway—just because we couldn't wait for them to ripen. Our favorites were striped June apples that ripened early, and we always had plenty of them. Mother would slice and fry them in butter and brown sugar, and we'd have fried apples and biscuits for breakfast. This is still one of my family's favorite breakfasts.

In summertime, we'd go to the creek and turn over rocks. We would catch the grampus (larvae of the stone fly) underneath. When we had filled a Prince Albert tobacco can, we would dig red worms and put them in another can. Then we would grab our cane poles and go fishing. We'd put the fish the boys caught on a small, forked limb we had cut off a nearby tree, running the limb through their gills and out their mouths. When we had enough for supper, we would take them home and clean them. Mother always fried them for us. Papa would sit at the table picking out the bones. He'd be so tired by the time he got all the little ones fed that he'd have to rest before he could eat his own supper. Over the years, not only did Mother fry our fish, she would also prepare whatever game Papa and the boys brought in—squirrels, rabbits, and now and then a turtle.

A hug from my pretty sister Cassie.

$\mathcal{W}$e didn't have many books, and we didn't have television, but we weren't bored, because we had Mother. She made us toys, rag dolls, monkeys, and little pillows from scraps of cloth. She made trains, doll houses, and furniture for our doll houses from boxes, spools, match boxes, oatmeal and cocoa boxes, and buttons. Then she would cut out paper dolls for us to play with in our doll houses. She would draw pigs, dogs, rabbits, and happy faces for us. She would save pieces of cloth, string, leather, and even corn silks for Papa to use, because he also made us toys. I

Mother in her record shop, which she and Dolly owned a long time ago.

particularly remember the stick horses, complete with tails and manes. He made us wagons, tractors, and little wooden guns. Yes, he made the girls wooden guns, too; otherwise, the boys would have attacked us and we'd have had no defense!

Mother helped us make playhouses in the edge of the woods near the house. We would choose a spot in the shade of a tree, then we'd mark off our "house." We would sweep the leaves and pine needles and then carry moss to put on the floor for carpet. We would use more moss for the beds and chairs. We decorated our playhouses with pieces of wood, rocks, and pine cones. Our dishes were broken pieces of bowls and plates. Sometimes we'd take the glass out of old discarded zinc canning lids and use them for plates. Our table was a piece of board set up on rocks and our tablecloth was a pretty piece of cloth from Mother's scrap box.

The brilliant orange blossoms of the chigger weed and the trumpet vine, along with the delicate white flowers of Queen Anne's lace, decorated my playhouse. Stella chose the blue chickweed and violets. Dolly always picked daisies and black-eyed Susans. Each of us had our favorite flowers, and we used them when they were in season. Stella liked the daisies, but

Dolly, who was older and bigger, also liked them, so she got to use them as "her" flowers.

So that we could continue our playing until the last minute, Mother would bring us dinner—sausage, bread, and cinnamon rolls or molasses sweet bread. She'd bring the younger babies with her, and they would be our dinner guests.

One might think, because there were so many of us, that we would have been neglected. But we never were. Our parents made the time to give attention to each of us. They always had time to listen to our dreams and encourage us. I can never remember feeling that our dreams weren't important, because to Mother and Papa they were.

Freida—what a pretty sixteen-year-old.

Doors and windows of the church were opened wide in the summertime to take advantage of any breeze. The lovely smells of mown hay and honeysuckle drifted through the open windows, creating an atmosphere totally different from that of colder weather, when we couldn't have the windows and doors open. The faint sound of a barking dog, a mooing cow, or the loud "eeee-ar-eeee-ar" of a jar fly vied for the attention of the congregation. Sometimes the preacher lost out to the sounds of nature! Bees and horseflies, and now and then an inquisitive dragonfly, wandered in and out of the pews as they pleased.

Church singings, with "dinner on the ground," are a tradition that has survived the test of time. Each family brings dishes of food to the church, and after the worship service, tables are put up outside. Sometimes the tables are nothing more than rough planks on sawhorses, covered with tablecloths. The women arrange the food on the tables, with the meat dishes placed together, the vegetables, desserts, and so on. If you've never attended a Sevier County dinner on the ground, you've missed out on some of the greatest food in the world. The women prepare and bring their specialties. I think the food tastes wonderful because of the enjoyment of being together, the comradeship, and the sharing. After everyone has eaten, the dishes and leftovers are gathered. Frequently the women exchange what they brought with someone else. Then everyone is ready for the singing. It is an afternoon filled with an easy, relaxed form of worship. Everyone is encouraged to sing, whether by themselves or in the congregational singing. We still have the old "harp singings," in which the congregation sings the sounds of the shaped notes, not the words.

In summer, we would sometimes go to tent revivals. The tent was always large and brown or dark green with ropes and wooden stakes that anchored it to the ground of an open field. Sometimes these revivals were held in early fall, when the nights were cooler. The field would have to be mowed, and the stubble mixed with the smell of the canvas tent and sawdust. No matter how carefully you walked, you got sawdust in your shoes. The canvas door was never securely tied back, and it always brushed our hair and clothes as we passed through. The men had to duck their heads and stoop to enter.

Once inside, we were completely surrounded by canvas because there were no windows. Usually four or five light bulbs hung on a cord from the top of the tent for light. The only outside light would be from a tear or rip here and there in the canvas. We enjoyed the tent revivals. There was something exciting about a church service in a tent, even if the benches and folding chairs were uncomfortable. The tent revivals are a thing of the past now, but they were popular in the fifties and sixties.

~

People all over Sevier County love to tease each other and laugh. To this day, Dolly takes this funny, childlike quality around the world as she performs. Outsiders enjoy getting an insider's view into our world, and our sense of humor is just one way for others to get to know us. But we have a serious side, too—a side that grieves when neighbors have hard times, a side that is strong in the face of trouble, and a side that helps people in need. When the aid is given, whether it is gathering crops for a man who's sick, taking food to a family that has none, or helping rebuild a house that has

Dolly signing an autograph for a fan.

Randy—a school picture.

burned, it's done with the words, "Don't thank me. I might need help someday, and you'd do the same for me."

The people who receive the help are made to feel secure and loved. The people of the county don't do these things because they think they have to, but simply because they *want* to.

The aid and comfort a family gives its members is an essential part of mountain life. As far as I can tell, it's always been that way—at least with our family. It's just another part of our mountain heritage. If someone is sick or in need, the family comes to the rescue, and it's not just immediate family but aunts, uncles, cousins—even in-laws! I've always known the old saying "We take care of our own" to be true. People remember the hardships they've been through themselves and try to make it easier for others. Mountain pride plays a great part in this, because it would be shameful for one part of the family to be destitute while others had plenty. Maybe that is why Dolly is so generous to her family, her community, and now the world.

When we were growing up our family did things for us, and we for them, over and over, making life much easier for all of us. Lots of friends did things for us, too. I remember Mary Carr. She worked in a candy store and she used to bring us large sugar sacks full of all kinds of fresh candy that was broken or wasn't cut or wrapped just right and couldn't be sold. Another neighbor, Odessa Messer, made cakes, cookies, and pies for us when she baked for her own family. She died a few years ago, and I cried for days over the loss of this warm, caring woman. Rachel Raines often helped me when Mother was sick

A passel of Partons. *Front row (left to right):* Cassie, Stella, Denver, Freida, Floyd, and Bobby. *Second row (left to right):* Randy, David, me, Rachel, Dolly, Mother, and Papa.

or had a new baby (which was often). Eunice Emert saved all her books and magazines, which she would bundle up and send to me. I didn't care how old they were, they were new to me. She also made delicious tea cakes for the children, who hurried to her house on Halloween to trick or treat. These are just a few of the women who taught me many important things about life, especially the necessity for giving and caring. I was just a young, skinny girl who needed help with my responsibilities, and they were the good women, sensitive and wise, who recognized my need and responded generously with their time and talent.

And there were others. Clyde McCarter used to buy toys for the smaller children. Randy was his favorite. He couldn't resist buying for the little blond boy with the twinkling blue eyes. Archie Ray McMahan and Nellie Fine gave us clothes, pieces of cloth, and whatever else they thought we could use. Clorine and Gaston Dockery always lived not far from us. They bought each of us a pair of little shoes when we were born. They even bought our brother Larry, who died as an infant, tiny, white silk shoes; and they went to the funeral home and put them on his feet. I don't know why they bought us our first shoes. I've never asked. But everyone in my family appreciates those fine people, who cared enough for twelve children to buy them twelve pairs of shoes.

The courthouse on the public square in Sevierville.

*T*he courthouse lawn, or square, has always been the hub of Sevierville, as it is in many small towns in the South. I remember going to town on Saturday and seeing the preachers on the courthouse square delivering sermons to the people standing in small scattered bunches. Some of the people were trading knives and watches, or trying to. A few of them would cast uneasy glances toward the preachers every now and then. There were small groups of women and men who listened intently, and "amen"-ed the preachers. A few women, caught up in the fervor of the sermons, shouted up and down the street in front of the courthouse.

The courthouse lawn was also used for stump speeches by political candidates. These usually drew bigger crowds and were a lot noisier because the crowds always joined in and gave their opinions. And sometimes the lawn was used by people who just had something to say that was neither political nor religious, but simply of concern to the community.

The courthouse lawn was used as a stage for singers and performers. Many gospel quartets have had all-day singings at the courthouse on Saturdays.

And many aspiring singers have performed under the huge oak trees that once had been used for hangings in the late 1800s. We didn't get to go into town often, but we looked forward to it, because "going to town" meant adventure and entertainment.

The pool hall was a dirty green building on Bruce Street close to the dime store. The door was two steps above the sidewalk. The lower halves of the two plate glass windows on either side of the door were painted green. There were usually two or three men or boys lounging on the steps watching the girls go by, and the heads and shoulders of several more could be seen through the upper part of the windows inside the pool hall.

Most women and girls wouldn't walk by the place and avoided it by crossing the street. When we asked our brothers what went on in there, they'd just roll their eyes and look mysterious. We'd always been told what a bad place it was and that no nice girls would walk by it, let alone speak to any of the boys who were hanging around it. When we were on the street across from the pool hall, we'd try to slip by without any of the "pool-hall crowd" seeing us, because they would whistle and nudge each other and snicker among themselves. It was embarrassing when everyone looked to see who they were whistling at! We'd heard about one of the braver Christian mothers who marched up the steps, past the shocked loungers, and into the pool hall to discipline a wayward son who was "hanging out" there. We had a lot of respect for that lady because she'd been in there, seen it, and come out again.

We know now that it was just a pool hall with nothing but chairs and billiard tables. It was mostly used by men who wanted to get away from their womenfolk. They're the ones responsible for the "den of iniquity" image. If we'd ever had the nerve to look at the characters on the steps or the ones looking out from the dirty windows, we'd surely have seen some of our cousins, brothers, and neighbors.

Another dreaded place in town was diagonally across the street from the pool hall, at the corner of Bruce Street and Court Street. This corner always had a group of older men gathered around, talking and spitting tobacco juice. When we came to that part of the tobacco-stained street, we'd hug the side of the building, trying not to walk in the tobacco spit and hoping no one would spit on us.

One Saturday afternoon in June, David and Denver hitchhiked to Sevierville, no doubt to hang around the pool hall and watch the girls.

Denver is ashamed of all of us from time to time, but that's never stopped us.

When they got to town they went their separate ways. Finally, it was getting late and Denver got a ride home with some of the guys from Jones Grove, a community near where we lived. He told them his brother needed a ride home, too. So they cruised town looking for David. They never found him and finally drove Denver home. About five o'clock in the morning, David came home. Denver was sound asleep. David pulled him out of bed, and they started fighting. They tore the house apart—even the stovepipe was on the floor. Papa got up and separated them, demanding to know what was going on. There they stood, Papa holding David—whose once nice white shirt and starched jeans were mussed and bloody—away from Denver—also mussed and bloody—wearing only the undershorts he had been sleeping in.

David told Papa that Denver had gotten a ride home and had left him in town, and he had had to walk the twelve miles home in the dark. Papa turned to Denver and said, "Is that true?" "Yeah," replied Denver. "I was ashamed of him. The guys drove by and, Papa, there he sat like a boll weevil in the courthouse yard with two of the ugliest girls I've ever seen! So I just told them I didn't see him anywhere."

The boys usually criticized each other's choice of girlfriends and always had bad things to say about our boyfriends. Ironically, we girls are still friends with our brothers' former wives and girlfriends. They will always be important to us and part of the family.

Above, front row (left to right): Uncle Orville, Aunt Christine, Uncle Winfred, Uncle Leonard. *Back row (left to right):* Papa, Uncle Earl, and Uncle Fred. *Below,* Papa, where did you get that outfit and that cigar?

Our dog Brownie.

We kids always managed to get cut on something or get a briar or splinter in our foot every summer. We would slip around, nursing our wound until Papa came home from work, because if Mother found out, she would *dig* the splinter out with a needle without fooling around. Then she'd douse the wound with alcohol or Merthiolate and say, "It's better now. Go and play." *Have you ever tried to play after putting Merthiolate on a cut?*

If we could escape Mother and her surgery until Papa got home, we were safe. He would make a big deal of taking out splinters. First he would hold the point of the sewing needle in the flame of a match to sterilize it. Then he would let it cool, and, working very slowly and carefully, he would remove the splinter without hurting us. Next, he would fix a pan of warm salt water to soak away the soreness. No alcohol! No Merthiolate! *No shock!*

Papa usually worked a job and farmed, too. When he would come home from work, all the younger children would run to meet him and raid his lunch bucket. We would swing on his arms, looking up at him and telling him all the exciting things that had happened that day. These simple acts provide us with some of our best memories.

In July, when the blackberries were ripe, all the kids would hunt up a lard bucket or an old syrup bucket for collecting berries. One or two of us could never find a bucket, so Papa would take a tin can, punch two holes in the top rim, put twine or wire through the holes, and make us a bucket, complete with a handle. Papa would rub coal oil (kerosene) on our shirt cuffs, collars, and ankles to keep us from getting chiggers. Then he would make us wait at the edge of the berry patch until he and our dog, Brownie, beat the patch for snakes. Brownie took his job seriously. When they got through with the patch there weren't too many berries left, but you can be sure that there weren't any snakes either. Papa wasn't as successful with the chiggers, though. Even with the coal oil, we managed to come out with a generous number.

When we were finished picking, we'd go home and show Mother and the babies how many berries we had picked. The older kids would tell Mother that this one or that one didn't do anything because they only had a few berries. She would settle it by saying, "I believe that's just enough for a pie." Or she would pour their berries all together and say, "Now, see how many all of you have?"

For a week, we would be busy picking berries to make jelly and jam, and we canned plenty of berries in half-gallon and quart jars. In the winter, we would have blackberry cobbler, and the juice was used a lot of times when someone was sick, like any other kind of fruit juice.

When summer storms came up, we had to run out and pick up chips of wood from the wood yard before they got wet. The hen that had been lying around under the boxwood bushes and scratching out holes in the dirt didn't know enough to get her baby chicks in out of the rain. We would run out and gather them up in our skirts and shirttails and put them in the woodshed until the storm was over. Sometimes we had hailstorms, and they were a

Uncle Leonard Parton with Cassie and me.

dreaded thing. We had to watch, unable to do anything, as the hailstones beat the leaves off our tobacco and shredded our garden and corn patch.

The summer days were long and busy. After supper in the evenings, we would all sit out on the porch in the cool breeze. We'd talk, watch for shooting stars, and sing. Mother would sing us all the old, sad songs that she knew. We would catch lightning bugs and turn them loose in our rooms to watch until we went to sleep. Our lives were full and happy.

When we got older, Dolly and Stella would come to my house for a weekend in July. We would make jelly and can vegetables from the garden. We'd make pickled beans and corn, and also kraut and cucumber pickles, for them to take back to Nashville. I only had one kraut cutter, so Dolly would take a Spam can and help me cut the cabbage while Stella packed it in crocks to ferment. We pickled our beans and corn in five-gallon crocks, too. We haven't been able to do that together for a long time now.

~

One summer, the boys did a little cooking and canning of their own. David and Denver were just in their teens, with Bobby a bit younger, but he was in on the hard work they were doing. All this ambitious activity had begun one day when they had been hunting and had stumbled upon a neighbor's moonshine still. There was no one around, so they really checked it out. David has a keen mechanical mind and the ability to draw. So he sat down and sketched a "blueprint." The boys slipped around for a couple of days, going back and forth from the still to see if they had drawn it correctly. Mother still has the blueprint.

It looked like they might never scrape together enough stuff to set up their still, until the brother of one of their best friends came to their rescue. Not only would he furnish the parts, but he also offered to give them sugar and anything else they needed, because he realized what an opportunity this was. He knew a good enterprise when he saw it. He could sell all the moonshine they could make in Frog Alley and pay them, too, and he knew that hard work was no stranger to my brothers. Well, before they knew it, their business was off and running!

That summer, for some strange reason, Mother was missing a lot of fruit jars—so many, in fact, that she had to buy extra jars for canning. All the while, the boys washed every jar they could find in the washtubs or in the creek by the still.

Mother didn't think it strange that they cut a lot of wood or washed a lot of jars, because they always did things like that. But we girls knew something was up, because they would disappear for hours at a time.

Randy. Looks like he's up to something.

My brother David and my sister-in-law Kaye.

We were so curious that we followed them one day, slipping through the creek and laurel thicket. When we came upon the still, we stopped dead in our tracks, wide-eyed and open-mouthed.

There they were, along with a neighbor boy, busy carrying water and stoking the fire. David was bending over, checking the run to see that everything was going right. He had on one of Papa's old blue work caps. Denver had on an old felt hat of Grandpa Jake's, which had a stain of sweat and grease around it from many years of wear. The neighbor boy wore a beat-up, misshapen straw hat. Bobby was there because the older kids had to look after the younger ones, and he was Denver and David's responsibility. Anyway, he didn't have a hat. They were all dressed in overalls and all, except for Bobby, were chewing tobacco and cursing. I have never seen them chew tobacco except when they worked on their still. They must have been copying the bootlegger. But we all loved to say bad words—so much so that when we were little, Mother made us a list of words we could use: John Brown, shucks, durn, and dadburn. But we liked the ones Papa said much better, and we used those when Mother and Papa weren't around.

Finally, we knew we couldn't wait and watch any longer. So we walked right up to the still. They looked scared when they saw us, and I thought they were going to run. David punched Denver with his elbow and said, "I'm glad you'uns came. We need you to taste this for us. We need an outside opinion." Denver joined in. He hurried and brought us a sip. Well, we drank and helped build up the fire. We couldn't tell on them, they reminded us often, " 'cause now we were guilty."

The still was in operation all summer until Papa got wind of it somewhere. One night at the supper table, Papa acted real upset that someone would tell such a thing on his boys. "Because I know," he told them, "that you wouldn't do such a thing." After that pronouncement, the boys took apart the still, and no trace of it was ever found. The boys were reformed, grateful for Papa's trust. They hunted, fished, and swung on grapevines. They caught unsuspecting June bugs, who didn't know it was August, and tied strings that Mother had unraveled from a bran sack onto the bugs' fat hind legs. Then they wrapped the string around the younger children's hands and the June bugs would fly

out the length of the string, scaring the smaller children if they lit on them with their little creepy, scratchy feet. The boys became somewhat better about helping take care of the little ones. And the girls kept their mouths shut, thankful that they weren't suspected of the part they had played in the operation of the still.

Papa where he likes to be—outside under a shade tree.

Dolly and Denver have always been cohorts. Years ago when we were children, Denver would hold court. He was always the judge (self-appointed, with Dolly's support). Naturally, he would allow only Dolly to be the jury. The rest of us were the criminals. We were found guilty of the most horrible crimes—horse stealing, murder, bank robbing, and running a moonshine still. Denver would preside over the cases, ask the questions, and pass out the sentences without bothering to listen to the criminals' defenses.

One of my worst crimes was making fun of Denver and Dolly when they had the "toe itch." This was a common malady for children who went barefoot in the summer. It was caused by a microorganism found in the dirt, especially in barnyards. The skin would crack open underneath and between the toes. The only cure we knew was to apply camphor or turpentine and tie a piece of wool yarn around the toe where the toe was sore.

This particular time, Denver and Dolly had it real bad on both feet. Mother had to tie up two or three toes for them, and Mother didn't tie a neat knot. She'd always leave an inch of the yarn dangling. The only yarn she had was bright green and orange. My brother and sister did look pretty funny, what with their shuffled walk, their intense pain, and their yarn-wrapped toes. I figured they deserved to be suffering, because they were always doing things to the rest of us. Well, my teasing them was evidently the worst crime that had ever been tried in Denver's court. He didn't sentence me to hanging ('cause I was bigger than he was), but to ninety-nine years of hard labor—no parole. I'm here to tell you that I'm still serving my time!

*O*ne of my family's favorite stories took place more than fifty years ago, when Papa married Mother one bright August day. Grandpa usually attended all the homecomings and singings in our area, and he always took his family with him. It was at one of these singings that Papa saw Mother for the first time. She was a pretty little thing, barely five feet tall, weighing less than a hundred pounds, and she had long black hair that fell past her tiny waist. Her skin, smooth and flawless, had never known makeup. She was shy and modest. Modesty was a virtue and Grandpa would tolerate nothing less.

During the singing, Papa watched Mother and listened for her alto voice that seemed to carry the other, weaker altos. By the end of the singing, Papa had made up his mind. He told the other boys, "I'm going to marry that pretty little black-haired girl." They laughed and hooted and hollered, "We'll just bet you are! Her father, being a preacher and all, will be real proud to have a good drunk like you in the family!" It was well known that Papa liked to drink, and he could pull some pretty good drunks. He could always be counted on to help a friend run off a few runs of moonshine, and if it had to be checked out to see if it was any good, Lee Parton was considered a good judge of whiskey.

Regardless of what the boys told him, Papa was in earnest. He knew he was going to marry Mother. He always seemed to be at her family's house after that. He helped saw and chop wood for winter, and he helped the Owens family plow their fields and plant crops that next spring. He was always there to walk Mother to church on Sunday. I know they made a striking couple: Papa, a tall blond with green eyes, dressed in a blue denim shirt and high-backed overalls, and Mama, so tiny that she could walk under his outstretched arm, dressed in a high-necked, long-sleeved dress.

Their love blossomed. Papa would sit and talk to Mother in the evenings, or at least he tried to, for when Grandpa was ready to go to bed, he would say, "Avie Lee, fix Lee a bed." This was a polite way of telling him it was time to leave, and Papa left in a hurry.

No matter where Mother would go, Papa seemed to be there. He was always sneaking looks at her, and Mother, though blushing, was of course looking back. During church services, Mother would go to the back of the church to

Papa and Mother out to dinner with friends at Stella's Hat House Cafe in Sevierville.

talk to Papa during the altar call. With her tiny hand on his shoulder, she would plead with him to go forward to the altar and give his soul to Christ. But Papa would mumble, "You just go on back up front, I'm all right." The young men mostly went to church to hear the singing and to see the girls.

On August 17, 1939, Grandpa, with his everlasting zeal, married them, hoping that Papa would settle down and become a Christian. He knew that Papa was a hard worker and had been all his life. Grandpa Jake knew that Papa would provide the best living he could for Mother.

The two young people walked down to the river. Standing straight and proud, they vowed their love and repeated the words that Grandpa read, words that made them man and wife. Papa, seventeen, and Mother, fifteen, certain that their love would last forever, could not know what the years would bring.

It had been raining earlier in the day and, as they walked hand in hand toward their future together, a rainbow appeared above the mountains. Papa teased his bride, saying, "Come on! Let's find the end of it so we'll have a pot of gold to start out on!" Mother pulled back on his hand. "No, Lee, let's just follow it at a distance and always keep it in sight."

Mother and Papa on a Sunday afternoon. They are probably wishing we all would leave so they could have some peace and quiet.

Bedtime came early in the hills, where work began at sunup. Papa knew all the beds would be full at his house, so he told Mother to wait outside under a window. In a few minutes she heard him say, "Catch!" and two homemade quilts fell into her outstretched arms. He came out of the house with milk, corn bread, ham, and a chunk of sweet bread (cake sweetened with molasses). Mother said, "I thought we were going to sleep here. That's what I told my folks." Papa just laughed. "And I told my folks we were going to stay at your house!" With his arm around her, Papa led her away. It was almost dark—that time of day when the mist is settling low on the ground and the moon is just beginning to appear over the mountaintops. As Papa guided her steps, Mother realized where they were going. The barn! She started giggling when she discovered where she would spend her wedding night.

They climbed the ladder to the loft and, in the middle of the loose, new-mown hay, they made their bed, laying one quilt down on the hay and folding the other one on top for cover. They ate their supper and then lay down in their marriage bed. Papa swears Mother was more afraid of the mules and cows in the stables downstairs than she was of him. She tells us that she was just glad they didn't have to sleep in the house with either of their folks, for they would have had to share a room with other members of the family. I think it was an exciting and pretty unconventional beginning, but then the rest of their life together has been that way, too.

For a few days they stayed with Papa's folks, and then Papa rented the Dennis place, which was miles away from any neighbors. The house, made of weathered gray logs, was small. The wood shingles on the roof were covered with moss and soft gray lichen. The house sat in a deep hollow; only the yard around the house kept it from being swallowed by the forest. Laurel thickets, with their rich green leaves, crept close to the house, their density almost engulfing the underbrush. In the sloping yard were remnants of daffodil foliage; red rambler rosebushes climbed everywhere. The branch (a small mountain stream created by the runoff of a spring) ran close to the house. Mint grew along its banks, filling the air with its pungent smell.

The little springhouse was built of logs and measured about six by six feet. The roof was made of moss-covered wood shingles. Inside it was dark and cool. The water ran cold and clean from underneath the ground. An old bullfrog was always sitting alongside the spring, as if keeping watch. There was a square trough built of rocks into which the water ran. Dishes of butter and crocks of milk were set in the trough to keep them cold.

Putting all their possessions into a horse-drawn sled, Mother and Papa moved into their first home. They took a wood cookstove, a bed, a table with two straightbacked chairs, quilts, two plates, two forks, two spoons, a butcher knife, and an iron skillet. Mother also had a few yards of cloth she would use to make curtains. She was a good seamstress, having learned to sew before she had gone to school. When she was a little girl, Mother had pieced quilt tops from scraps of cloth. It was a blessing she could sew, because she had many years of sewing ahead of her. Little did they know what a large family would grow from their humble beginnings.

Mother and Papa
catching a quick kiss.

Papa and Hannah.

A couple of years ago Dolly invited all the nieces to her house for a slumber party. The girls had packed bags to spend the night with their Aunt Granny (Dolly). They had had a busy day already. Hannah had been diagnosed a year earlier with leukemia. Her treatments were going well but some days she just didn't feel good. Hannah was tired and a squabble broke out among the girls. Dolly, trying to settle it the best she could, made Hannah angry—even more angry than she already was at the other girls. In a last retort she told Dolly to call her mother to come get her, she wasn't staying another minute.

Hannah put her clothes in her little suitcase, carried it to Dolly's back porch, sat down on it, and waited for Rachel. Dolly and the cousins tried to talk her into rejoining them. She wouldn't.

It took Dolly quite a while to get Rachel. In the meantime they all realized they were hungry, so Dolly made macaroni and cheese. Hannah wouldn't join them to eat. Dolly, in a last effort at making a peace offering, said, "I'll just leave it here with you, maybe you will want it later." Still concerned, Dolly kept checking on her from behind the kitchen curtains. Dolly said Hannah would eat a little from time to time after looking around to see if she was still alone. Rachel finally came and rescued all of them.

Hannah had told Dolly she was never going to forgive her, plus a few other things. As time passed, she refused to let it go, and she stayed mad at her Aunt Granny no matter what Dolly did to make amends.

When Hannah got real sick again and Dolly was visiting her, Hannah was still cold toward her. Dolly couldn't stand it any longer. With tears in her eyes she told Hannah that she had to forgive her. Hannah was ready to give it up anyway, I suppose. But all she said to Dolly was, "We'll just forget it." And they have.

Hannah loving her teddy bears.

Hannah can forget almost everything now connected with her illness except during the few seconds several times a day when she takes a handful of medication. This is always done without a comment from anyone, and Hannah never complains. She was told early in her treatment that in order to get well she had to take her medication as it was prescribed, and Hannah has too many things she wants to do not to get well.

Often, when she would have to go "to clinic," as she called it, she would pack a bag of her favorite things—a little Bible, the quilt Mamaw Parton made for her, a doll Papa gave her, a toy truck with her treasures in it. Aunts, uncles, cousins, and friends had all given her small gifts. Of course, she just dragged me along in person, as well as her mother and father, Rachel and Richard.

Some of the less conventional things she took made it only to the parking lot—a puppy named Sarah, a ferret named Cloey, and various hamsters. "Eggie," a baby iguana, actually spent the day in the clinic once. The staff and nurses had suspected she had something, because she kept having me check the backpack. She was told that live pets were not allowed in the hospital, so for some time after that she enjoyed pretending she had an animal in her backpack, just to get a reaction out of the staff.

This little donkey named Dolittle didn't want to go on the wagon train, but Randy and Mitchell did.

During warm weather, the family children always like to camp and hike with me. The wagon trains are the best treat of all, I think. Not very long ago we camped most of the summer and had took lots of nature walks. My nieces Heidi, Hannah, and Rebecca call these "hiking picnics" or "mountain climbing." They all especially needed this time with each other and Mama Deene (me).

At the end of the trip, we came into the house with a load of dirty clothes from our camping and hiking. We all smelled like horses, because we had spent days on the local wagon train. Someone had set out a picture of me that the girls hadn't seen before. They said, "Oh, Mama Deene, is that you when you were young?" I just dropped my camping bag and kept walking toward the shower. I hollered back, "That was me before the wagon train!"

I keep a petting zoo at my farm for the children—Hannah has a horse named Kenny's Sunday Kisses, a goat Sylvia, and a lamb Casey. All the children have their own pets. Rebecca has Sugar, a horse. Her pig is named Cynthea, and her lamb, Kista. Heidi had Valentino, a lamb. Valentino had been born with lung problems and only lived about a year. Heidi's heart was broken, and so was ours. He was the most beautiful Jacob's lamb anyone had seen, with truly gorgeous markings. Now she has Little Dipper's Dream Catcher, a horse—a paint with a mark on her hip in the shape of the little dipper. She also has a new lamb named Kissyfur. She has Sarah, the dog, who has accompanied Hannah to treatment. We had to take trips to the parking lot all during the day to check on Sarah. She was usually sleeping in the van and would get up for hugs and treats, and to take short walks.

On the farm we also have dogs, cats, goats, sheep, calves, horses, rabbits, and a raccoon: Hobo, Back Pack, Amber Feathers, Handsome, Romeo, Katy, Dude, Midnight, Lightning, Boudrow, Zeus, Spot, Boat, Angel, Snowball, Snowflake, Sam, Jake, Bijou, Blackberry, Callie, Dobber, Little Man, Be Bop, and Branden. And, of course, we have fish, some named, some not.

"What do I do now, Mama Deene? I'm out of feed."

Then there is Wonder, a calico cat that just showed up at my door one day when the children were visiting. Wonder was ready to have kittens, so we all went into high gear making a place for her to have her babies. The girls kept feeding her and checking on her and asking me, "Please, Mama Deene, can we keep her?" So of course I said yes. They were excited and said they would call her Wonder. When I asked why, they said it was a wonder I let them keep her and that she had just "wondered" into our lives. Randy and Heidi took her with them after a few days. They live only a few houses down the road with Bubba, their dog that also "wondered" in a few years ago, and another cat.

Top left: Our Jacob lambs (bible sheep). *Top right:* Hobo. *Bottom left:* Sylvia and Angel. *Bottom right:* Little Dipper.

Freida and Floyd at seventeen.

*R*ecently I was organizing various family papers and I ran across this letter written by Freida to her brother Floyd when they were both seventeen:

To Floyd, my closest relative and friend,

You are a part of me, you are my twin. I have nothing to leave you or give you but these few words that I'm writing you for your birthday. We were born into a family of love, to the two most wonderful people in the world. I guess you and I have a closeness not shared by the other brothers and sisters, because we are twins. I hadn't realized how close we really are until this year, being apart. Floyd, I guess you and I should thank our lucky stars and our God for the family we were fortunate to get born into. Sometimes just looking at a certain flower, a sunset, or sunrise, even a drop of rain, makes me realize these things. I can't say what I really want to or how I feel inside, but at least you know I'm trying. I wish you lots of luck and happiness on your road to fame, and I know you will make it. Everybody knows you are the best writer in the family. They all say so.

Happy Birthday from your twin,

Freida Estelle Parton
June 1, 1974

*O*ur niece Dena and our cousins Tammy and Tammy's daughter, Cassle, wanted to be baptized one summer. They wanted to be baptized in the river that runs by my cabin in North Carolina. They, Mother, some friends, the minister, and Dena's baby, Jordan, came early one Sunday morning. The baptizing was to be at four P.M. I had served brunch, complete with cut flowers and white candles. It was a great day. There was a table with white linen for the sacramental wine and unleavened bread for the service. The table also held the family Bible and a book for recording the names of the newly baptized.

Suddenly it started storming, as it sometimes does in the mountains. The fishermen started leaving the river banks. Two of them had promised to stand by in case we needed them at the baptizing. I had asked them because it didn't look like any of our men would get there in time. My mother, the Reverend Annie Mae Denton, and her sister, Mary Lou, are elderly ladies and can't swim. I can't either. Therefore I had asked the fishermen to be there for our safety. One of the guys came to the cabin and said, "I don't believe you ladies need to have your baptism today. This river rises rapidly when it storms." Well, he was right. The river rose and turned dark and loud. The girls were so disappointed.

I felt that if they wanted to be baptized that much, I needed to find a way. I got my umbrella and told them I'd be back soon. I figured there had to be a motel nearby that had an indoor swimming pool. The first motel I came to had two pools, one inside and one in the back, nestled into the mountain. They offered us the empty one, out back. A few people gathered around, and that only added to the beauty of the event. The sun had started shining again, and the girls had one of the most memorable baptism ceremonies our family has ever seen.

Our whole family lives in the shadow of a song. And songs have seen us through some really hard times. Most of our children are better than average singers. Our five youngest often have sing-alongs. Jada, Tever, Heidi, Rebecca, and Hannah—they all sing even when they're alone. They sing with anything—music on the radio or television. And they sing with Aunt Granny's (Dolly's) tapes, and Freida's, Randy's, Rachel's, and Stella's tapes. So they get a lot of practice.

Nieces and nephews playing in Mother and Papa's yard.

I vividly remember one day when Hannah was about midway through her intense chemotherapy for leukemia. She would frequently sing on the way to and from the hospital. This summer day she had asked me to ride in the back seat with her. Sometimes she wanted her mother, Rachel, and sometimes she wanted me. Richard, her dad, almost always drove when he was with us, which was most of the time. He would carry her to and from the car when she was not able to walk. This day was one of those times.

Her hair had fallen out by this time, and she was very swollen. One of the medicines made her hungry and angry most of the time. As we drove to the hospital for more treatments, she asked us how many angels we thought were in the sky that day. We said we didn't know. She said, "A hundred?" We said maybe. "A thousand?" she said. We said maybe. The sky was a gorgeous blue, with fluffy white clouds moving along with the wind. She said, "My Grandpa Jake is up there, and my Daddy's grandpa. You and Mama have a baby brother up there, too, don't you?" I said we did, that his name was Larry. The clouds looked liked angels flying along. She said, "I know how many angels are there. Mamaw says we have ten thousand angels just watching over us, and I bet we have a bunch in this car right now." I told her I was sure we did.

She had to have a lot of things done that day—a spinal tap, blood work, and a bone marrow tap. It was bad. As Hannah was getting blood work done, Richard left the room for a few minutes. Just as he returned, Hannah screamed. Her father froze. He just stood there with tears running down his face while she cried pitifully. He couldn't bring himself to go back in, and I couldn't blame him.

Whenever she was getting ready for the spinals and bone marrow taps, she always wanted Rachel to sing to her. Hannah would hold onto her mother tightly as she sang. Rachel would sing two songs; one was "Michael, Row the Boat Ashore," and the other was one that Rachel had written.

Finally, when we left late that day, Hannah wanted "chicken on the bone," as she called a drumstick from Kentucky Fried Chicken. She ate a couple of bites and handed it to me to put back in the box. Richard had laid her in the back seat on a pillow, with a blanket. She had her feet in my lap and she wanted her feet massaged. She requests this of Stella, Richard, and me all the time. She says she is trying to see who is the best.

Suddenly Hannah started singing a song I'd never heard before. It was new. I don't know whether Rachel and Richard had heard it or not. They just held hands and looked straight ahead as she sang. I held her and I looked out the window. She sang these words twice, then fell asleep:

> That was a river, this is the ocean
> That never carried this much emotion.
> Nothing compares to this deep devotion.
> That was a river, this is the ocean.
> The love we had before can never change this one;
> We're not imprisoned by the past we brought along.
> It's just you and me, one ship in the night.

(Hannah raised her hand and pointed her finger at each of us, then herself.)

> There are no boundaries; there is no end in sight.
> That was a river, this is the ocean
> That never carried this much emotion.
> Nothing compares to this deep devotion.
> That was a river, this is the ocean
> Nothing compares to this deep devotion.
> That was a river, this is the ocean.
> That was a river, this is the ocean.

Left to right: Hannah, Richard, and Rachel.

When we got to the house, Rachel jumped out of the car and ran to unlock the door. Richard picked up Hannah. She put her arms around his neck, patted him on the back, and said, "Daddy, I love you." He said, "I love you, too, baby girl." I hurried toward the trash can to get rid of cups, napkins, and chicken on the bone. We never mentioned that day to each other, or any of the other sad days, while she was so sick.

Now Hannah is well and has grown tall. She has lots of pretty hair again and acts more like a teenager than a seven-year-old. When I look at her, so healthy and happy, I think about all the people who prayed for her, and how we were all sustained by the power of such prayer and the mysterious gift of music in our lives.

Even at a young age, Mother taught us about God, religion, and keeping the Sabbath holy. Both our parents emphasized the importance of always "doing right," as they called it. Papa says he has never prospered when working on Sunday, and sometimes he would even get hurt when doing so. Once, right after he and Mother married, he broke his leg on a Sunday logging job and was housebound for a couple of months. Another Sunday, not long ago, he was making toys for some of the kids and he cut two fingers with a skill saw.

One time, when we were young, Papa sent Bobby to replant corn in the back field. We were living at the old Oliver place, in the Caton's Chapel community. Bobby poured a little bag of corn in a big stump that had been there for some time. He threw a few handfuls of dirt over it, and off he went, with his dog, King, to fish.

He remembers he had a very good day. He saw a lizard on a log. He saw a water snake slither away under the water. He caught white suckers, fish, from under the bank of Byrds Creek, where water gnats were darting about in a pool near the edge. He remembers wondering where they thought they were going. He remembered a blue-and-white snake feeder (dragonfly). He wondered why they were called that. He knew for sure they didn't feed snakes. But a snake might feed on them if given the chance.

Bobby and King. When King had a broken leg, Bobby took very good care of him.

A few weeks later, Papa was doing his usual checking of everything at home while he was off work over the weekend. He found a stump with thick corn growing profusely from it. He came back to the house, picked up two hoes from underneath the front porch, and said to Bobby, "Son, I guess we better check out our corn. It should be about ready to hoe by now." Bobby said, "Daddy, it's Sunday. I'll do it the first thing in the morning." Papa said, "No, we'd better get to it."

They walked to the back field, Papa and Bobby each carrying a hoe. Faithful King walked close to Bobby. When they got to the edge of the field, there was very little corn to be seen. Bobby stood there with his hand on King's head. He was the only friend Bobby felt he had in the world, and Bobby knew King couldn't help him this time.

Bobby said, "Daddy, the crows must have eaten this bunch of corn, even with all the tin pans and scarecrows hanging in the field." (The pans make noise when the wind blows. A scarecrow is made to look like a person standing in the field and usually has a shirt and hat belonging to a family member.) Papa took Bobby to the stump, lit a cigarette, and stood there, watching him squirm.

Later we asked Papa if he whipped Bobby. Bobby said, "Why are you asking him?" We said, "Well, did he whip you?" Bobby said, "Yes, he did, but the whipping didn't hurt as much as Papa making me tell him in detail everything I had done. We walked through the whole thing again, step by step. Then he told me the whipping was going to hurt him more than me!"

We never did quite believe that one. We did learn at a very early age, however, that you can't do wrong and get by—not at our house anyway.

Papa's family. *Front row:* Great-grandpa Huston and Great-grandma Tenny. *Back row (second from left):* Grandpa Walter Parton.

*W*hen we were kids, our friends ate things like cotton candy and popcorn balls. But not us! We preferred purple and yellow salt blocks, which measured about a cubic foot. They were put on a short stake in the pasture for the cattle to lick. The yellow ones contained salt and sulphur and the purple ones were salt and minerals. We loved them! We'd carry a piece around for days, licking on it. When Hubert Whaley and Clyde McCarter put up new salt blocks, we would beat the cattle to them. Clyde finally caught some of us chipping off pieces of his new salt blocks, so he came to our house and told Papa. Papa didn't believe him and was upset that anyone would accuse his children of eating the cattle blocks. We sat there wide-eyed, our pockets bulging with chips from Clyde's salt blocks. Even today we have cattle, horses, goats, and sheep, *and* we have salt blocks. Believe it or not, they still taste good!

Mother and Papa worked hard all summer long. We children would sit under the apple tree peeling fruit, breaking beans, shucking roasting ears, or chopping cabbage. If we weren't done when it was dark, we just moved the whole mess into the house and worked there. Mother and Papa canned jars and jars of food. We would build a fire outside and use the washtubs as kettles. We would place the jars of food in them, fill the tubs with water, and cover them with a piece of tin. It took four hours to cook each run of beans. Mother and Papa also took rancid lard from the smokehouse and made lye soap in the big iron kettle outside. When the soap was cool and hard, we would cut it into squares. Then it was ready to use for washing dishes and clothes, for scrubbing floors, and for taking baths. We also used it for shampoo. We worked hard and nothing was wasted. Those times were sometimes difficult, but they were always good. They made us strong and resilient. Many people today are poorer for not being able to live in such a way that draws them closer to the earth, and closer to each other.

∾

Our family reunions are usually held in conjunction with decoration days at certain cemeteries. We've always loved Decoration Day in Sevier County, when you visit old friends and remember the ones who lie in the graves. People come from all over the region to put flowers on their loved ones' graves. Each cemetery has a day set aside, such as the last Sunday in May or the Sunday closest to the thirtieth of May. This way, everyone knows when to expect Decoration Day at their particular graveyard.

For weeks before Decoration Day, the families used to spend evenings making crepe-paper flowers to decorate the graves of their family and friends. The petals of different shapes and sizes were carefully cut out of the sheets of colored crepe paper. We would curl the petals by putting them between our thumb and one cutting edge of the scissors and then pulling the petal through as we applied pressure with our thumb. The flowers were created by following a printed pattern. They were put on a piece of special wire about eight inches long; the wire was wrapped down about three inches with green crepe paper; and leaves were added. Sometimes we dipped the finished flowers in hot wax to make them strong enough to last outside for months. We sometimes experimented and created new patterns of our own

Left to right: Mother, Janet, Papa, Donna, Dena, and Heidi. Amanda is in front.

"Pretty Miss Dolly," as Porter would say.

design. We made iris and apple blossoms. We even tried marigolds. My favorites were the roses and tulips.

Then real roses, lilacs, day lilies, and zinnias were gathered by the boxful. We liked wild flowers, too, mostly daisies and cornflowers (bachelor buttons that used to grow wild in the corn fields). These flowers would lie alongside the crepe-paper flowers and the bright plastic flowers and wreaths that are so popular today. Come next Decoration Day, the stark, lonely graves with marble and gray slate headstones will be transformed once again into a garden of colors.

Political elections in Sevier County are enjoyed by young and old, by the losers and the winners, but most especially by the supporters of the winning candidates. For months before the elections, hopeful candidates and their staunch supporters go from door to door and from farm to farm giving the residents a small card with the candidates' names and pictures, and sometimes a list of their qualifications.

In the county election, the most intense campaigning comes in the races for sheriff and road commissioner. Then come the district constables and school board members.

Arguments and debates take place everywhere—from country stores and barber shops to the courthouse lawn. The pros and cons, the issues and rumors, are discussed with fervor, and sometimes fists.

The political issues take a back seat to the personalities of the candidates. There is plenty of mudslinging, some of it true, some of it not. The closer to election time, the shorter the tempers. The supporters are sometimes more serious than the candidates.

Many election promises are made; few are kept. Candidates for road commissioner promise good roads. Candidates for sheriff promise law and order. Tax assessors promise lower taxes.

I remember when one candidate for road commissioner asked an older man to vote for him for a second term in office. The campaigning took place in Cleo McMahan's grocery store. There were quite a few people in the store, and the man's voice was loud and clear. "I don't guess I'll vote for you. You might take a notion to fix our road and our geese would be pretty mad 'cause they've made nests in the holes."

When we were young, election day was always exciting for everyone, from the oldest to the youngest. Children who didn't know the issues knew who was in their parents' favor or who was the worst person running for office.

Nobody worked on the farm on election day. It was a holiday observed by everyone who could vote, and even those who couldn't. I remember those hot August election days, when it almost never rained. I think high spirits must have kept the clouds away.

Someone—a candidate or supporter, usually—would eventually get around to offering to buy everybody lunch on election day. A person would always be asked at least three or four times, "Have you eaten dinner yet?" Some candidates would have a truckload of watermelons to serve anybody who wanted a slice. One of my brothers would always end up bringing home a whole watermelon.

We'd slip around and listen to the men standing in crowds, talking and passing out " 'lection liquor," especially to the men who hadn't voted yet. The candidates would get a few children together and give each one of them a handful of cards to pass out among the crowd. This usually earned us a dollar or two each. What they didn't know (or did they?) was that we'd take cards from both sides. We'd pass out one candidate's cards for a while and then pass out the other's.

One time I made the mistake of telling on my Papa and two of my uncles. After I had walked home from the school where the election was held, Mother asked, "Did you see your Papa anywhere? He was supposed to come and take me to vote hours ago." I told her, "Oh, yeah. He and Uncle Fred and Uncle Lester were talking to three women when I left."

Mother and one of my aunts started out of the yard toward the school at the same time. She yelled back at me, "Willadeene, you stay here with the babies until I get back." I guess they rescued the men that time because sometime later they came riding back to the house with Uncle Lester and Papa.

*W*e knew that if we didn't keep cats, we would have rats. So we always had a couple of gray or calico cats that were constantly winding around our legs and getting under our feet. When Papa thought we weren't taking care of them, all he would have to say was, "All right, kids, if you don't feed your cats, they will leave home and the rats will eat us alive." We'd heard crazy stories about rats biting little kids and we were scared to death of them; so we made sure to feed the cats until they were so full they couldn't leave. I guess rats were the only animals we didn't like.

There was a family of skunks that passed through our barnyard every day. One day we lay in wait for them, for we were always catching baby birds, squirrels, or rabbits but we had never had baby skunks to play with. We got them! But the mother skunk didn't take kindly to kidnappers. Her aim was good, and she sprayed us all. When Mother found out, she made us turn them loose. Then she washed us, using canned tomato juice, and burned our clothes.

Our hearts were broken. We hadn't had the time to really enjoy our new pets. Mother just didn't understand! So we sat by the roadside waiting for Papa, to tell him of our awful troubles. He often took our part when Mother handled our tragedies. All the while he was taking our part, he'd wink at her over our heads to let her know that he agreed with her, but we needed a friend.

We left our doors open in the summertime, and the flies came and went at will. So we had to use flypaper. Every house had flypaper strips inside, and outside on the porches. We don't see them much anymore because most houses have screens, and insecticides are plentiful. A flypaper strip was a sticky piece of paper two inches wide that was tacked to the ceiling and hung down. It was about eighteen inches long. The paper was so sticky that if you touched it, it left the gum on your hands. When flies lit on it, they couldn't get loose. It served its purpose, but it wasn't a very pretty sight, because it was left hanging until there wasn't room for another fly. Then it was taken down and another one was tacked up.

Flies weren't the only thing that wanted to get in our house during the summer. Old setting hens would wander up on the porch with their brood of fluffy chicks following right behind them. The mother hen would hop up in the doorway and cock her head from side to side, surveying the room. When she was satisfied, she'd walk boldly into the house and cluck for her little chicks. They'd come running with their stubby little wings raised like they could fly. They'd wander from room to room behind the mother hen until her curiosity was settled. Then they'd go back outside.

We once had a game hen that flew through a broken window in the attic and made her nest on a feather bed. When the chicks hatched, there was no way she could get them down. So we rescued the babies and brought them down to her in a basket.

Dolly and Clint. "Oh, Aunt Granny, stop it."

*E*ach year, Mother and we girls take a vacation. It is so secret that not even our husbands and children know what we do. The existence of these vacations has come out in some of Dolly's interviews, but she has never given away any of the details. Here is the diary I kept when Mother chose the theme and location of one of our trips.

Tuesday

I got up early today because I was too excited to sleep. We're having our yearly get-together: Mother, Dolly, Stella, Cassie, Freida, Rachel, and me. For a whole year we've planned for this week. I wanted to get my house cleaned up real good before I left, but I had too much company and too little time. I did get lots of food cooked for Mitchell and his dad, and also some to take on our vacation.

Cassie and Stella called about five o'clock from Cassie's house in Alabama. They told us that they were going by Dolly's house in Nashville to pick her up and then come on home to Sevierville. They still don't know what Mother has chosen for our vacation; I'm the only one who knows because I helped her get ready. They tried to get me to tell them, but they should know by now I won't.

It was close to midnight when they finally got here. Dolly got in the house first. She loved the way Mother was dressed for the occasion—an old red dress pinned with safety pins in front where the buttons were off and her headscarf tied like Aunt Jemima's.

We visited with Papa and the rest of the family for a few minutes, then we got our things together and went to the cabin. The cabin isn't far from where Mother or I live, but everyone knows that they can't intrude. This is our special time together.

Mother carried a flashlight for us to walk by. We all tried to stay close together, for it was pitch dark. Mother had been to the cabin earlier in the evening and built a fire in the old mud-daubed fireplace and lit a couple of lamps and a lantern. We could see a faint light through the windows, but Mother had covered them with black shades so no one could see inside our place (and so we could sleep in the morning if we stayed up late).

Mother loosened the big skeleton key from her dress where she had pinned it and unlocked the door. She stepped back so we could see what she had done. Even I was surprised, and I had been helping her with a few things when she needed me!

Dolly dropped her guitar to the floor and the rest of us sat down. There were squeals and squawks as six grown women went from room to room exploring the old place. And then, silence, as we realized that the place Mother had chosen for us to spend our vacation was our childhood!

Supper was on the wood-burning cookstove; its aroma filled the little house and it sure made us hungry! We had meat loaf, green beans, potatoes, hot biscuits, and an old-fashioned apple stack pie.

As Mother set supper on the table, we girls began exploring. We found two old trunks, but she wouldn't let us look inside. She had papered the walls of the cabin with newspapers and cardboard, and hung old family pictures of distant relations and some ugly and funny ones of us. She had Dolly's first picture when she went to work for Cas Walker on the mantel over the fireplace. We discovered the mantel held more treasures of the past. There were old tin tobacco and snuff cans, sticks of licorice candy, bubble gum, peppermint candy, some Blue Waltz perfume, Rosebud salve, and Juicy Fruit and teaberry gum. Everyone kept saying, "Oh, Mama! Oh, Mama! All the work you've done for this!"

During our discoveries, Mother was busy putting our supper on the old table that was covered with red oilcloth like we used to have. The kerosene lamp sat in the middle of the table among jars of homemade jelly, pickles, and relish. She built up the fire a bit and acted like she wasn't even listening to us.

After supper we sang a lot of old sad songs and some funny songs. Four of us sang tenor on the same song! We decided we had a pretty good tenor quartet. We soon tired of the songs, and decided to try to go to bed.

Mother had three beds in the front room. She'd made straw ticks for our beds and we had feather ticks over that. We'd drunk two pots of strong coffee made on the open fire, and when bedtime came, we couldn't go to sleep. So we talked about a lot of good people and included a few bad folks, too. Some of us pulled the covers over our heads pretending we were ashamed.

Stella decided that if there was one among us who was good enough and hadn't gossiped she should pray for the rest of us. No one volunteered. So everyone went to bed saying their own silent prayers—at least I know I did!

P.S. It was six A.M. when we went to bed.

A picture from our vacation. Dolly is trying to make Mother laugh.

Wednesday

Mother was up first, making our breakfast. Dolly and Stella pretended they were rich little girls having orange juice and toast before starting their day of leisure, reliving a childhood fantasy. They looked so silly because they were drinking from pint Mason jars and eating out of pie tins. The table was set just like when we were growing up.

After breakfast we went outside to a beautiful day with the sound of summer everywhere—birds and frogs. And from somewhere across the hills, we could hear a rooster crowing and the hungry bawling of a new calf.

It was just cool enough for light jackets. Dolly had brought all of us new ones made in the "Coat of Many Colors" style. She had gotten them from fans when her song "Coat of Many Colors" became a hit. All of them were handmade and beautiful. A lady in Texas made the one I wore. Her name and address were on a tag sewn inside the jacket.

We spent the rest of the day visiting friends, neighbors, and relatives. We went to our old homeplace on Webb's Mountain and visited our friend Hubert

Everyone in our family loves Dolly more than anyone could believe. I am so proud of our family. Our people are kind, caring, good, and gentle, and no one shows this more than Dolly.

—Aunt Dorothy Jo

Whaley and his sister Hazel, who live there now. On our way home we stopped by Aunt Exa McMahan's country store for ham and bologna sandwiches and Moon Pies. We visited a while with Aunt Exa and Uncle Cleo. Then we went to see Bob and Addie Allen, Vic Webb, Aunt Lillie Huskey, Lillard Sutton, Pink Parton, Perry Lindsey, and Uncle Phillip Owens, who gave us a small token to take home.

We went for a long, long walk. Later Cassie went with me to pick up Mitchell from school because there was no one else to do it today.

Stella and Dolly had fixed supper when we got back. They even made a pan of corn bread with cracklings. For dessert we had banana pudding. They announced as soon as Cassie and I came through the door that we could do the dishes because they had done the cooking. They are both good cooks but Dolly messes up the kitchen something awful!

We'd invited Papa to stop by and eat with us on his way home from work. He looked so tired. He had been pouring finishing concrete alongside David and Denver on the construction job where they all work together. Papa washed up for supper in the wash pan on the side porch. Dolly and Cassie combed his dark blond hair, and Dolly told him she and Stella cooked his supper. Dolly petted him and said she thought she would look like him if only her hair were curly. She talked about how she used to sit on his lap and comb his hair over to the side trying to get it not to curl so much. Daddy said the house reminded him of some of the first places he and Mother had lived. Dolly told him she had a painting made of a pair of his old working boots she had asked him for. Dolly taped all of the conversation while Papa was there. Cassie and Papa didn't talk much, but they never do.

Dolly went out to a pay phone in Pigeon Forge to call Carl and to check on Mrs. Dean, her mother-in-law. She has been sick for a few months and Dolly worries about her.

Mother finally let us open the two old trunks. We had never seen the dark green one before we got to the cabin. She told us she got it from Phoebe Messer for five dollars and that Perry Lindsey or Pink Parton was going to refinish it for her. The other trunk, a black one, belonged to our great-grandmother Louisa Valentine. It's bigger than the green one, and they're both pretty large. We opened them and they smelled of cedar and mothballs. They were filled with wonderful things! There were old love letters boys had written us that went something like this:

Dear ———

    How are you? I am fine. I hope you are fine too. I like you. I hope you like me too. Are you mad at me? I am not mad at you.
Love,

———

P.S. I like you better than ———.

    There were valentines, candy boxes shaped like hearts from our sweethearts, Christmas card boxes full of letters, and cards from boyfriends. There was a comic book that had belonged to a boy Dolly liked. It had "Dolly and Wayne" written on it. (I wonder if he still remembers the green birthday cake?)

    Mother had kept the cards, letters, and jewelry I had gotten from a boy named Carl, and a valentine and a ring from Lynn. I confided to the girls that Lynn was the first boy I ever kissed and how I thought he was so-o-o good looking. There was the blue dresser set Earl had given me and a blue bottle that had been from a set of Evening in Paris perfume my husband had bought me before we were married.

    After a bath to wash away all the dust and memories, we put on long dresses and fixed up like Southern belles, complete with parasols. We decided to go to the church house where Grandpa Jake preaches and sing for a while, where we'd have a piano.

    Aunt Estelle and Dorothy Jo were visiting Grandpa Jake so they joined in the singing. Neighbors who heard the music came in and listened and we visited with them. When we were through and went back to the cabin, Estelle and Dorothy Jo went with us.

    We reminisced about when we were little, and we asked them about Mother when she was growing up. We love to hear about our parents when they were children. We got tickled when they told things on Mother. I guess she's always been pretty independent, and we do love her so.

    Dorothy Jo had gotten comfortable on one of the feather beds and didn't want to get up to eat supper at the table. She was propped up on pillows with her banjo, writing a song. So we catered to her lazy whim and carried her supper to the bed on a tray.

    When we were ready for bed, Mother had put a surprise just under the covers. When we pulled them back we found the old *True Story* magazines we thought she had destroyed when she caught us reading them years ago. Finally, after twenty years, I got to finish the story I was reading when she caught me. (We always suspected Mother read them herself.) We even play-acted how she would snatch them from us and then slip off and read them. It was hilarious! Then we all sat up in bed and read them until we were almost asleep.

Good night, dear diary, and . . . *True Story*.

A family homecoming. *Left to right:* Stella, Freida, and Dolly.

Friday

This morning we got up early and dressed in jeans and flannel shirts for a long day in the mountains exploring old buildings and sawmills. Dorothy Jo didn't have the ambition to go so she spent the day with Mother. But Estelle went with us. I think that this day will always stand out in my mind as perfect. We took pictures and strolled through old graveyards where a lot of the graves were marked with gray slate rocks for headstones. We climbed over and under rail fences and wire fences.

We took turns carrying the lunch Mother had fixed. We ate early so we wouldn't have to carry it any longer. We had potted meat, biscuits and ham, fudge, crackers, raisins, soda pop, and two oranges that we peeled and shared.

On the steps of the old empty cabins, we sat and talked and wondered and even made up stories about all the people we imagined might have lived there.

I hated for evening to come, but the magic of the day lingered for us all.

Tonight we gave Mother, Dorothy Jo, and Estelle a surprise tea party. We had made a lot of teas from all kinds of herbs and spices, but we served real sassafras tea tonight.

Each of us girls wore one of Dolly's wigs (and fixed our makeup like hers). It's funny to see six Dollys! We took turns dressing like each other. Sometimes there were six Willadeenes or six Stellas or six Cassies. It is so funny that we can actually look like any one of our sisters.

We gave Mother, Dorothy Jo, and Estelle each a nightgown, a pink one for Mother, a red one for Dorothy Jo, and a blue one for Estelle. We each tried to tell them how much they mean to us and how we love them, but there is no way we can ever hope to express the depth of our love. We gave up and just hugged and kissed them and went to bed.

Saturday, our last day

Stella left early and picked up her son, Timmy, at Darlene Williams's house. She was going to visit her in-laws here in Sevierville and some of her friends. Cassie, Dolly, Estelle, and Dorothy Jo got up before daylight. They woke me up but I didn't let them know because I didn't want to see them leave; I was afraid I'd cry. Cassie and Dolly kissed me goodbye. After they were gone, I went back to sleep.

Mother and Papa's baby child and our sweet sister, Rachel.

Mother was gone when I finally got up. She went home to fix Floyd, Randy, Freida, and Rachel's breakfast. The cabin was warm, but the fire was going out and it was lonesome. So I grabbed my things and took a last look around and left fast . . . probably never to have as good a time together again . . . and for sure not in the same place or doing the same things. Each one of us has a year to plan the vacation for the others, and each vacation is different. This had been Mother's year, and who else could plan a vacation in the past?

Our vacations are times set aside for love and sharing; times when the outside world doesn't exist. Yet the world is blessed with the songs and music and poems and stories that are born at these times, or later, in the remembering.

~

There is a reason and a season for all things. I truly believe this. For this book there was the sowing, then the growing. This book has been growing, tucked away in my heart for years. We're continually shaped and rearranged. Hearts are made softer, we hope, and time teaches us many things. Sometimes I feel I am being guided by an unseen hand, as I feel we all are. Without my family and the inspiration and exasperation we provide for each other there would be no book, no songs, no plays for us. We are playing our lives out on a stage or screen for the world to see, to laugh or to cry with us. I'm sure God planned it that way, so that surely makes it all right with us.

The Next Generation of the Parton Family

Bryan

Janet

Mitchell

Dena

Donna

Misty

Amanda

Jordan

Nora

Tabatha

Danielle

Jennifer

Clint

Chris

Heidi

Tever

Tim

Rebecca

Hannah

Jada

Dollywood Lights

Words and Music by
RANDY PARTON and
DEB PARTON

Verse

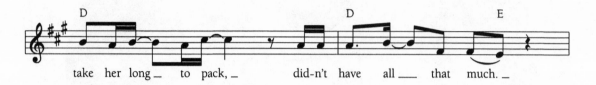

Leav-in' town on a Grey - hound bus, Did-n't

take her long _ to pack, _ did-n't have all _ that much. _

Suit - case full of songs and a beat-up old _ gui-tar, _ A wild _

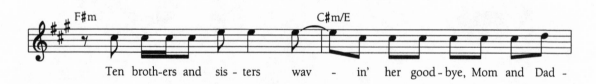

_ i - mag - i - na - tion that was gon - na take _ her far.

Ten broth-ers and sis - ters wav - in' her good - bye, Mom and Dad -

dy hold - in' hands, _ With tear - drops in their eyes, As she rolled _

Chorus

_ in - to the night, tail - lights fad -

ing out-ta sight, _____ With star -

dust in her eyes _____ and Nash -

ville on her mind. _____

2. Woke up in Nashville not knowin' what lay in store,
   Down on Music Row she knocked on ev'ry door.
   When one man answered, her songs were on the air,
   Duets of heartaches, other dreams they didn't share.
   Rhinestone rainbows, the Grand Ole Opry stage,
   "I will always love you and I'll be back someday,"

Second Chorus
   As she rolled into the night, Music City fading outta sight,
   With stardust in her eyes, and Hollywood in mind.

3. L.A.X., the "sandman" met her flight,
   Said, "You're gonna be a star, girl, and see your name in lights.
   She's made the movies, the "walkway of the stars,"
   But those mountains keep on a-callin' and tuggin' at her heart.
   Angel face in tight denim jeans
   Lookin' past the tinsel in her "white limousine"

Third Chorus
   As she rolled into the night, on down Hollywood and Vine,
   With stardust in her eyes, and Dollywood in mind.

4. Carousels spinnin', there's miles of Christmas lights,
   Smoky Mountain magic just seems to come alive.
   Arts from the past and a coal train engine roars,
   And on the wings of an eagle hearts begin to soar.

   Always met with a handshake and a grin
   And that "homespun fun" 'll make you wanna come back again.
   Stars of tomorrow at Dollywood today,
   Singin' their hearts out up there on her stage

Fourth Chorus
   Under those Dollywood lights, that's what Dolly had in mind,
   And the lights as bright as Dolly when she smiles.

Until We Are Old

Words and Music by
WILLADEENE PARTON and
FLOYD PARTON

for - ev - er and ev - er

you'll _ be sat - is - fied. _____

Hold me and love me, _____ don't ev - er let _

go. _____ Make me your _ lov -

er _____ till we are _ old. _____

2. You understand me like no one else can.
   I'll be your woman, always be my man.
   I'll never need another, you're the only one for me.
   You are my darling, only one I need.
   (Repeat Chorus)

Nickels and Dimes

Words and Music by
DOLLY PARTON and FLOYD ESTEL

1. I used to stand __ on the cor - ner when I ___ was a child, And I'd play my gui - tar and sing as the peo - ple went by. The side - walks were crowd - ed, but I'd just sing loud - er 'cause I did - n't mind. Just spend-ing my time, __ spin-ning my rhymes __ and sing-ing for nick - els and dimes.

Chorus

Nick-els and dimes, __ a song at a time ___ for nick-els and dimes. __

I'd bright-en their day __ as they go on their way and they'd

bright - en mine. __ A side-walk re - hear - sal for

dreams that I held __ in my mind. __ I

knew that some - day __ in my own spe - cial way __ I'd re -

pay all their nick – els and dimes.

2. I recall the sidewalk each night as I stand on the stage,
As I play my guitar and sing for the people who paid,
'Cause I finally made it to what they call the big time,
But I still remember I still owe some nickels and dimes.

Second Chorus
Nickels and dimes, a song at a time for nickels and dimes.
A sidewalk rehearsal for dreams that I held in my mind.
So, if you remember a child on the corner of time,
You'll know that I wrote this to repay your nickels and dimes.

Smooth Talker

Words and Music by
STELLA PARTON and FLOYD PARTON

Verse

1. You walked in-to the room in your flash-y west-ern clothes, Tall, lean, and hand-some, that's for sure. And as you turned to me And as your eyes met mine, I knew you could talk me in-to your arms.

Chorus

Oh, smooth _____ talk-er, won't you tell me what I need to hear. And, smooth _____ talk-er, come sit down o-ver here; You're a smooth _____

talk - er, yeah, I know you're a la - dies' man, But I'll

take you as you are, ___ If you'll just take me as I am.

2. Let's sit and talk a while; I'll take that glass of wine.
   You tell me your story; I'll tell you mine.
   Yes, you can take me home, If you'd like to spend the night
   For I can't stand the thought of being alone.
   (Repeat Chorus)

3. The morning brings the sunlight and the memory of love lost.
   Love that was willing and so warm
   Now we both know the score; We needed love and nothing more;
   I'll admit love was good inside your arms.
   (Repeat Chorus)

Pretty Lies

Words and Music by
FLOYD ESTEL and FREIDA PARTON

She's gon - na cry be - fore the morn - ing, __

__ She's gon - na cry _____ through the night _____

__ She's gon - na cry _____ be - fore the morn - ing _____

__ When the morn - ing comes _____

who'll dry her eyes _____ His pret - ty lies.

He al - ways pro - tect - ed her, He told her pret - ty

lies _____ When it came down to leav - ing her, he

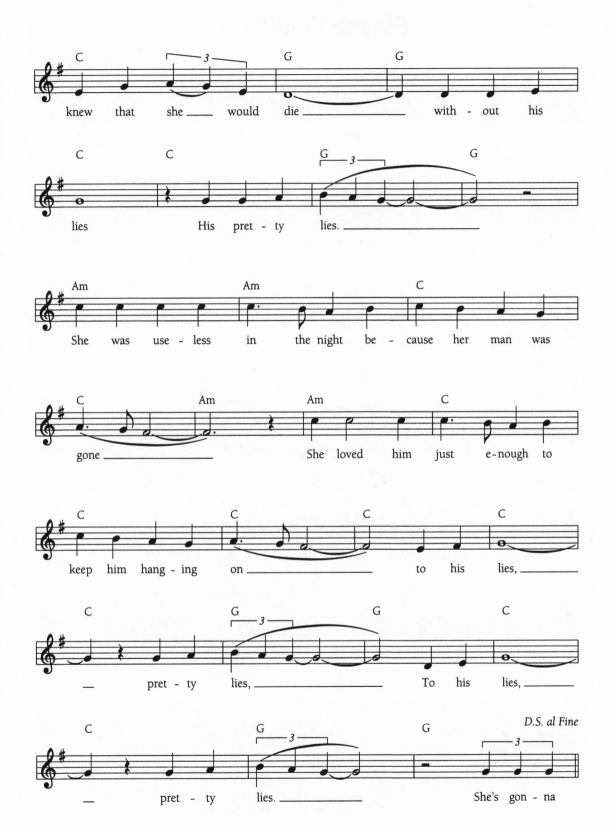

D.S. al Fine

227

Please Don't Lie

Words and Music by
RANDY PARTON and FLOYD ESTEL

Verse

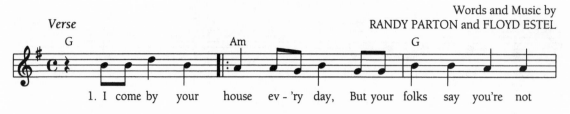

1. I come by your house ev – 'ry day, But your folks say you're not

home.   I know bet – ter, 'cause I hear your voice When I

ring you on the phone.   *Chorus* Please don't

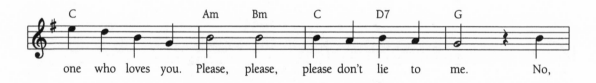

lie,   don't make a fool out of me; Don't lie,   'cause I'm the

one who loves you. Please, please, please don't lie to me.   No,

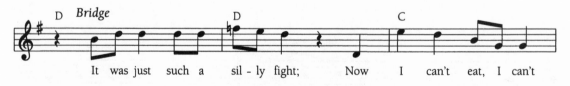

no, don't lie to me.   2. That's the thing, the

Bridge

It was just such a sil – ly fight; Now I can't eat, I can't

sleep at night.   Love   can   turn   you   in - side   out;   You

took   me   in,   and   you   turn   me   out. _____

2. That's the thing, the thing about love.
   Sometimes falls down from above,
   Send your heart, heart in a whirl,
   When you find that special girl.
   (Repeat Chorus)

3. If we could just talk it over,
   If we have to, we could start all over
   I am sure I can make you see,
   If you'll just talk to me.
   (Repeat Chorus)